THE JESUS LIBRARY
edited by Michael Green

The Hard Sayings of Jesus
F. F. Bruce

The Teaching of Jesus
Norman Anderson

The Supremacy of Jesus
Stephen Neill

The Empty Cross of Jesus
Michael Green

The Counselling of Jesus
Duncan Buchanan

The Example of Jesus
Michael Griffiths

Jesus: Lord & Savior
F. F. Bruce

The Evidence for Jesus
R. T. France

The Healings of Jesus
Michael Harper

THE JESUS LIBRARY
Michael Green, series editor

The Evidence for Jesus

R.T. France

INTERVARSITY PRESS
DOWNERS GROVE, ILLINOIS 60515

For David and Sue

Published in the United States of America by InterVarsity Press, Downers Grove, Illinois, with permission from Hodder and Stoughton Limited, England.

InterVarsity Press is the book-publishing division of InterVarsity Christian Fellowship, a student movement active on campus at hundreds of universities, colleges and schools of nursing. For information about local and regional activities, write Public Relations Dept., InterVarsity Christian Fellowship, 6400 Schroeder Rd., P.O. Box 7895, Madison, WI 53707-7895.

Cover illustration: Janice Skivington

ISBN 0-87784-986-2
ISBN 0-87784-933-1 (The Jesus Library set)

Printed in the United States of America

British Library Cataloguing in Publication Data

France, R. T.
   The evidence for Jesus.—(The Jesus library)
   1. Jesus Christ.—Historicity
   I. Title.   II. Series
   232.9′08   BT303.2
   ISBN 0 340 38127 8

Library of Congress Cataloging in Publication Data

France, R. T.
   The evidence for Jesus.

   (The Jesus library)
   Bibliography: p.
   Includes index.
   1. Jesus Christ—Historicity.   I. Title. II. Series.
   BT303.F77   1986   232.9′08   86-20927
   ISBN 0-87784-986-2 (pbk.)

18	17	16	15	14	13	12	11	10	9	8	7	6	5	4	3	2	1
99	98	97	96	95	94	93	92	91	90	89	88	87	86				

Editor's Preface

It is a matter of amazement to me that books constantly get published, and television programmes produced, which set out the most bizarre interpretations of Jesus of Nazareth on the most slender of evidence. Jesus Christ maintains the astonishing fascination he has always exercised; but, as ever, men and women are reluctant to face up to the challenge of his claims and the cost of discipleship. In self-justification, they tend to show an incurable preference for inferior evidence, or else a determined scepticism towards the New Testament records.

Dr France is a very able New Testament scholar, and he is well aware of these tendencies. He also knows that no amount of evidence will convince those who are determined not to see. But in this very clear and well organised book he outlines the evidence, Christian and non-Christian, which undergirds the Christian claims. Coolly and succinctly he surveys what the New Testament and Gentile writers, Josephus and archaeology, Qumran and the Gnostic Gospels have to tell us about Jesus. He is not, of course, out to give us yet another 'Life' of Jesus. But he does set out, in its entirety, the evidence on which we are challenged to make up our own minds about Jesus. And in my judgement he brilliantly succeeds.

I commend this book, by a fair minded and distinguished New Testament scholar, to Christians and non-Christians alike. Here is one part of the evidence about the most amazing and influential person who ever walked this earth. The other part is provided by the worship and devotion of

that third of the human race which acknowledges him as
Lord. If we are prepared to weigh this evidence with integrity
we shall be driven to make our response to the question
'What do you think of Christ?', and live with our decision. I
fancy the author would not ask for more.

MICHAEL GREEN
Series Editor

Author's Preface

When Michael Green originally asked me to write this book for the 'Jesus Library', I was reluctant. It would mean delving into areas with which I felt too little acquainted, and I was not sure that I relished the thought of further acquaintance. And who would read such a book anyway? Were there not plenty of books already available for those with such off-beat interests?

Then, just as I was trying to reconcile myself to the task, Channel Four screened a series, *Jesus – the Evidence*, to which reference will be made later in the book. Neither Michael nor I knew this series was forthcoming at the time when the book was planned, but it could not have been more timely. The widespread interest and concern which those programmes aroused showed me, as no arguments by the series editor could do, that there was a real need for such a book – and there might even be potential readers! At the same time my own interest was stirred up, as I was asked to participate in discussions arising out of the television series and realised how fundamental were some of the issues it had uncovered.

So the book has been written, and as I have worked on it my reluctance has evaporated, until I almost regret having finished it. I have enjoyed some (for me) new discoveries, and a fuller and more purposeful encounter with subjects and documents I had known only casually before. The scope of the book does not allow me to share all this with the reader, but I hope there is enough here to convey something of the pleasure and renewed confidence I have found in reinvestigating the essential foundations of Christianity.

Where appropriate I have included extracts from the relevant sources in English translation. In most cases the translation is my own; where I have used a published translation,
this is acknowledged in the notes. Biblical quotations are
generally taken from the RSV, though occasionally I have
supplied my own translation; no attempt has been made to
differentiate them in the text.

This book has more extensive notes than most in the 'Jesus
Library'. While I did not wish to encumber the text with a lot
of references which most readers would want to ignore, one
cannot honestly present 'evidence' without indicating where
that evidence is found. And in the hope that at least some
readers will share enough of my fascination to wish to pursue
the subject further than a short book like this allows, I have
offered in the notes some guidance for fuller reading.

DICK FRANCE, June 1985

ABBREVIATIONS

BJRL   *Bulletin of the John Rylands Library*
CBQ   *Catholic Biblical Quarterly*
EQ   *Evangelical Quarterly*
ERT   *Evangelical Review of Theology*
Ex.T   *Expository Times*
IEJ   *Israel Exploration Journal*
JBL   *Journal of Biblical Literature*
JJS   *Journal of Jewish Studies*
JTS   *Journal of Theological Studies*
NTS   *New Testament Studies*
Nov T *Novum Testamentum*
TDNT   *Theological Dictionary of the New Testament, G. Kittel*
       (ed)
TynB   *Tyndale Bulletin*

Introduction

Jesus was a common name among Jews in the first century AD. In Josephus' history twelve different individuals carrying that name are mentioned in that century alone, including four of the high priests. The popular hero Barabbas was, according to the most likely reading of Matthew 27:16–17,[1] also called Jesus, so that Pilate's question to the crowd was a puzzled (or perhaps ironical?), 'Which Jesus do you want, the son of Abbas, or the one who is being called Messiah?'

But among all the Jesuses of the time, only one is now remembered, and the name 'Jesus', for us, refers only to him. This Jesus, and the movement which he founded, has become so central a part of world history that it is a shock for us to realise that if you had said 'Jesus' to almost any Jew of the first few centuries AD it would have been no more specific than 'George' might be for us, and it is very unlikely that if he did think of a specific individual it would have been the one we call 'Christ'.

Centuries of Christian devotion have encouraged us to assume that 'our' Jesus was as conspicuous a figure in his day as Napoleon was in his. And they have woven around him a composite character as 'Lord', 'Saviour', 'King of Kings', 'Son of God' (often with the subconscious addition of the features and character of a medieval Italian saint or a Renaissance monarch) which suggest something different from the Galilean preacher whom Pilate sent to his death instead of Jesus Barabbas.

This tension between popular devotion and historical reality has proved a powerful attraction to those who wish to uncover the 'real' Jesus, and present him, perhaps to the embarrassment of the faithful, as a three-dimensional man of his time.

I believe this is a healthy and proper desire. If there is popular superstition and pious misinterpretation in many people's conception of Jesus, it is surely in nobody's interest that it should be allowed to persist unchallenged. Unfortunately, however, the search for the 'real' Jesus depends on a proper assessment and an appropriate application of the evidence available, and it is here that the ways begin to diverge. The end result is a vast range of different Jesuses, and the claim to scholarly objectivity soon begins to wear thin.

In recent years there has been a steady stream of unconventional portraits of Jesus, mostly produced with at least an appearance of careful historical scholarship, though few, if any, by specialists in New Testament studies.

Undoubtedly the most courageous is G. A. Wells, Professor of German at Birkbeck College, London, who has for years been insisting that Jesus never existed, but was a mythical figure arising out of Paul's mystical experience, for whom an earthly 'history' had later to be invented. Wells' books[2] are written with a painstaking attention to detail and a calmly rational tone, but his method is that of a man who knows where he is going, and who therefore always selects from the range of New Testament studies those extreme positions which best suit his thesis, and then weaves them together into a total account with which none of those from whom he has quoted would agree. We shall refer later to Wells' arguments particularly with reference to the force of the non-Christian evidence for Jesus, but his position as a whole is fanciful.

Even more bizarre was the theory of John Allegro, a Semitic scholar, who argued, apparently seriously, that Jesus was originally a cipher for a sacred hallucinogenic mushroom around the use of which the Christian cult first arose.[3]

Few of the 'reconstructions' of Christian origins in recent years reach quite such a height of absurdity, and most do at least acknowledge the existence of the Christians' Jesus as a real person, however different he may have been from the traditional image. Some have cast him in the role of a failed Zealot leader.[4] In similar vein is the theory of H. J. Schonfield[5] that Jesus engineered his own 'crucifixion' and 'resurrection' in order to establish his claim to be the Messiah.

Even more offensively to many Christians, Morton Smith has presented Jesus as a practitioner of magical rites, with sexual overtones.[6] We shall meet this charge, in a less extreme form, in Jewish anti-Christian polemic of some centuries after the time of Jesus, but Smith is seriously suggesting this as the true historical assessment, which he bases on 'suppressed evidence'.

Most recently, an even more extraordinary reconstruction has been published as an 'explosively controversial international best-seller' (so the publishers claim) under the title *The Holy Blood and the Holy Grail*.[7] Its authors start from medieval traditions connected with the Cathar sect in south-western France, and weave around these an amazing collection of esoteric material from quite diverse sources which range from ancient Gnosticism to Rosicrucianism. They thus 'discover' a secret society dedicated to the restoration of the Merovingian dynasty in France, and proceed to trace that dynasty to the direct descendants of Jesus, whom they suppose to have been married to Mary of Magdala; Mary, they suppose, brought their son (hence the 'Holy Blood') to Marseille, and this is suggested as the basis of the later legend of the 'Holy Grail' (Saint Gréal = Sang Réal, 'Royal Blood'). The whole thesis is constructed by an imaginative exploiting of 'coincidences', often quite superficial, between unconnected traditions.

It is tempting for those who move in more traditional Christian circles to dismiss such apparently perverse 'reconstructions' of the 'real' Jesus as unworthy of notice, mere aberrations on (or beyond) the fringes of recognised biblical scholarship. But they show no sign of going away. Indeed there is currently in North America quite an upsurge of such thinking, with the avowed intention of supplanting the traditional understanding of Jesus with an alternative based on

reputable scholarship. This has been for several years a
prominent focus of the magazine *Free Inquiry*, leading to an
'International Symposium on Jesus and the Gospels' held at
the University of Michigan in 1985 under the title 'Jesus in
History and Myth'. That conference, which featured several
of the names mentioned above, was sponsored by *Free Inquiry* as part of its 'Religion and Biblical Criticism Research
Project' which aims to foster such alternative accounts of
Christian origins. The writers whose work has appeared in the
magazine in this connection represent a variety of viewpoints,
some avowedly humanist, others 'liberal Christian'. Their
suggested reconstructions differ from one another. But all are
united in the conviction that the Jesus we thought we knew
from the gospels does not represent a real figure of history.

All such reconstructions of Jesus necessarily have in common an extreme scepticism with regard to the primary evidence for Jesus, the canonical gospels, which are regarded as
a deliberate distortion of the truth in order to offer a Jesus
who is fit to be the object of Christian worship. Instead they
search out hints of 'suppressed evidence', and give a central
place to incidental historical details and to later 'apocryphal'
traditions not unknown to mainstream biblical scholarship,
but which have generally been regarded as at best peripheral,
and in most cases grossly unreliable. The credulity with which
this 'suppressed evidence' is accepted and given a central
place in reconstructing the 'real' Jesus is the more remarkable
when it is contrasted with the excessive scepticism shown
towards the canonical gospels, a scepticism which has often
been declared no less than perverse by historians and literary
critics in areas outside biblical scholarship.[8]

A primary aim of this book will be, therefore, not merely to
list the various types of evidence for Jesus available to the
historian, but also to bear in mind the relative value to be
attached to the various types. It is obvious that the most direct
and explicit evidence for Jesus comes from the four canonical
gospels. Such evidence must surely take a central place in
reconstructing the facts about Jesus unless it can be shown to
be unreliable or even deliberately misleading. A good part of

the book must necessarily be devoted, therefore, to assessing the value of the gospels as historical evidence. If they are accepted as substantially reliable, all other evidence must necessarily find its place in the context of the framework which they provide. It is only if the gospels are found to be unable to bear this historical weight that there can be any justification for building one's portrait of Jesus on hints of 'suppressed evidence' and on inferences drawn from the wider historical scene.

This is not to suggest, of course, that even if the gospels can properly be taken as the foundation for our knowledge of Jesus, there is therefore nothing to be gained from other, perhaps non-Christian, sources. On the contrary, one of the most exciting features of recent study of the New Testament has been the way in which new light is constantly being thrown on aspects of the life of Jesus by the study of the world in which he lived. In particular, the increased study of Judaism of the Roman period has led to some important clarification of much of our understanding of Jesus. Traditional ways of envisaging the gospel scenes have been altered, and Jesus has increasingly come into clearer light as a man of his times. As we learn more to see him as a contemporary Jew would have seen him, we may expect to come closer to the real Jesus. If in the process we lose some of the stereotypes which have made Jesus for many a blue-eyed Caucasian with the values and attitudes of a middle-class Englishman, this is not something to be regretted. In the final chapter of this book we shall return to this aspect of the search for the 'real' Jesus.

At Easter 1984, British television screened a series of programmes entitled *Jesus – the Evidence*, whose avowed aim was to use the findings of modern historical research to shatter the conventional image and to begin to rebuild a picture of the historical Jesus who might turn out to be very different from the Jesus most Christians thought they were worshipping.[9] Some of the theories mentioned above, and others in a similar vein, were given prominence in this series, while the canonical gospels were, by and large, not treated as serious historical evidence. The series posed questions rather

than confident answers, but the clear intention was to indicate
that whatever the truth about Jesus may have been, it was
certainly not consistent with later Christian devotion to him as
the Son of God.

The series was greeted by a storm of protest. Much of the
protest was justified, because the one-sided nature of the
scholarly opinions presented was obvious to anyone who
knows what is happening in wider scholarly circles today.
Some of the purely speculative reconstructions floated in the
series verged on the irresponsible. But it would be a pity if this
failure to do the job properly were taken as an indication that
the job should not be done at all.

This book is not designed to respond to that series, which
will probably have been generally forgotten long before this
book is published. But the controversy it aroused well illustrates both the importance and the sensitivity of our subject –
and at the same time warns us that a claim to be following 'the
evidence' needs careful evaluation. For while undoubtedly
that series did present some evidence relating to the historical
Jesus which was both valid and potentially enlightening, the
truth of the picture which emerged was radically affected both
by the selection and relative weighting of the evidence
offered, and by the interpretation which was placed upon it.

This book, then, will not be another attempt to reconstruct
the 'real' Jesus (though some pointers in that direction will be
offered in the final chapter), but will go further back to discuss
the nature of the evidence on which such a reconstruction
must be based. It aims to describe, and to evaluate, the
different sources with which a historian must reckon, and to
assess the different types of evidence they offer. Inevitably in
the process some judgements must be made as to where, if at
all, the various pieces may fit into the structure of a well-
balanced account of Jesus, and of where the main outlines of
that structure are to be sought, but this is not the place to flesh
it out into a finished portrait, even if such a task could be
regarded as ultimately possible.[10]

In speaking of 'the historical Jesus' and of the work of 'a
historian', I am well aware that for many people Jesus is not

just a historical figure. For most of them historical evidence is not what matters most, even though they would find the suggestion that their understanding of Jesus was 'unhistorical' both offensive and disturbing. The root of their acceptance of Jesus is not historical study but present experience, an experience which is no less real and convincing for being labelled 'subjective', and which is the more impressive when that 'subjective' experience is found to have been shared, with a rich diversity of individual expression, with multitudes of followers of Jesus for many centuries, and shows no sign of disappearing from the contemporary scene as one of the most powerful motivating forces in the world. But that too is another subject. I have no wish to decry that sort of evidence for Jesus; indeed if the account I will be offering of the historical evidence is true it would be surprising if there were not such experiential evidence of a Jesus more 'real' than a dead figure of the past. I believe that there is no fundamental discrepancy between these two types of evidence; rather each reinforces the other. But they are not to be confused, and my brief in this book is to deal with that type of evidence which falls within the province of the historian.

Chapter
1

Non-Christian Evidence

The first thing to be said about non-Christian historical evidence for Jesus is that there is not much of it, at least from a period close enough to the events to be of any value as an independent witness to Jesus as seen through non-Christian eyes. It is often suggested that this fact is very damaging for the New Testament portrait of Jesus: it lacks external corroboration, and is therefore suspect.

This impression is strengthened by the instinctive assumption of many Christians, which we noticed in the Introduction, that Jesus was a historical figure of such universal significance that, like Napoleon, or Gandhi, he must have left his mark on the life and writing of the men of his day far outside the circles of his immediate followers. You could scarcely have lived in the Roman empire of the first century, it is assumed, without being aware of Jesus, even though they lacked the saturation coverage available through the modern communication media. Surely any well-informed man of the day must have had his own views about Jesus, and must have discussed him in the social gatherings at the baths. And of course no responsible first-century historian could avoid devoting a respectable slice of his work to Jesus and the Jesus movement.

But it does not take much reflection to realise that this is quite the wrong scenario. For one thing, the availability of international news in Jesus' day was not the same as it is for us, or even as it was in the days of Napoleon.

For another thing, much of the historical and other writing of the period has not survived. For example, even the great histories of Tacitus, to which we shall return, have survived in only two manuscripts, which together contain scarcely more than half of what he is believed to have written; the rest is lost.

But the most important fault in this view of Jesus' historical significance is in the character of the events themselves. Galilee and Judaea were at the time two minor administrative areas under the large Roman province of Syria, itself on the far eastern frontier of the empire. The Jews, among whom Jesus lived and died, were a strange, remote people, little understood and little liked by most Europeans of the time, more often the butt of Roman humour than of serious interest.[1] Major events of Jewish history find their echo in the histories of the period, but was the life of Jesus, from the Roman point of view, a major event? The death of a failed Jewish insurrectionary leader was a common enough occurrence, and religious preachers were two a penny in that part of the empire, a matter of curiosity, but hardly of real interest, to civilised Romans.

F. F. Bruce, in his important study of *Jesus and Christian Origins outside the New Testament*,[2] to which we shall have cause to refer frequently in this chapter, offers a suggestive parallel in the history of 'The Fakir of Ipi', a holy man and popular leader in the India of the British Raj who achieved occasional mention in the British press, but 'I do not suppose that he will play a prominent part in histories of the twentieth century'.[3] The fact that Jesus, unlike the Fakir of Ipi, became the centre of the world's greatest religion does not require that during his (short) life he would have been any more noticed in the world's press or its history books. It is only as the religion which he founded began to spread and to win significant numbers of converts outside his native Palestine that we might expect to find it (and therefore, by implication, its founder) beginning to figure in the literature of the Roman empire. And that, as we shall see, is precisely what we do find.

But if the pagan world of the Roman empire might not be expected to find much cause for concern in a Jewish preacher, at least we might expect to find some reference to him in Jewish writings of the period. Yes, indeed. But the problem is that not many Jewish writings of the period have survived. Those which might be expected to contain any reference to

Jesus fall into only two categories. Firstly, the massive histories of Josephus, written towards the end of the first century; and secondly the traditions of the words and deeds of the Rabbis, which were mostly not compiled in writing until long after Jesus' time, but which do contain what some scholars regard as substantially authentic (if fragmentary) accounts of some prominent first-century religious figures. And in fact both of these sources do yield some material about Jesus, though in each case there are problems about both its reliability and its interpretation, resulting from the peculiar literary character and history of the writings concerned.

It may help in assessing the significance of this non-Christian evidence if we look at it in three categories. First we shall look at what I have called 'direct reference to Jesus', by which I mean passages which refer to Jesus himself as a historical figure, or which may be interpreted as doing so. Then at 'indirect evidence', by which I mean early references by non-Christians to the Christian movement, in which Jesus figures not so much as a historical figure in his own right but rather as the central figure of the religion. Finally we shall consider 'background evidence', material which we may call on not to tell us anything directly about Jesus or Christianity as such, but to provide the setting within which the historical reality of Jesus must be understood.

A. DIRECT REFERENCE TO JESUS

1. Gentile writers

Only one pagan writer in the century following Jesus' death offers us an explicit reference to him as a historical figure. That is, of course, Tacitus, whose *Annals*, probably written shortly after AD 115, include a brief mention of Nero's persecution of the Christians at Rome in AD 64. The relevant passage runs as follows. Nero is himself suspected of having started the great fire which damaged Rome in that year:

> To dispel the rumour, Nero substituted as culprits, and treated with the most extreme punishments, some people, popularly

known as Christians, whose disgraceful activities were notorious.
The originator of that name, Christus, had been executed when
Tiberius was emperor by order of the procurator Pontius Pilatus.
But the deadly cult, though checked for a time, was now breaking
out again not only in Judaea, the birthplace of this evil, but even
throughout Rome, where all the nasty and disgusting ideas from
all over the world pour in and find a ready following.

(Tacitus, *Annals* XV. 44)

As evidence for the existence of a significant Christian
community in Rome in the mid-sixties, this is an important
statement (particularly as the tone of Tacitus' language
makes it quite clear that he himself had no bias in favour of
Christianity!). But more important for our purpose is the
account of 'the originator of the name'. Tacitus gives us his
name ('Christus'), his home (Judaea), his date (the reign of
Tiberius, AD 14–37, and more specifically the governorship of
Pontius Pilatus, AD 26–36),[4] and the fact that he was executed
by order of the Roman governor. This is hardly an impressive
biography, but it does apparently serve to earth Jesus firmly in
contemporary pagan history. It would seem that here all
attempts to prove that Jesus never existed must founder.

But G. A. Wells[5] is not dismayed. After all, he points out,
what matters is where Tacitus got this account from. His
report is certainly good evidence for what was generally
believed about the origin of Christianity in Rome at the
beginning of the second century. But does this reflect
any more than what Christians were saying at that time
about themselves? Wells will happily agree that the figure of
'Christus' (notice that the 'historical' name Jesus is not used,
only the title by which Christians referred to him) as a real
person executed by Pontius Pilatus was part of Christian
tradition by the end of the first century, but he argues that this
in no way requires that that tradition was based on historical
reality. In other words, Tacitus' recording of Christian beliefs
about their origins has no independent value as evidence for
what actually happened. There is no reason to believe that he
had access to any official records, only to the popular understanding of the origins of Christianity.

For the lack of any official record of the trial and death of Jesus, and for early attempts to fill the gap by both supporters and opponents of Christianity, see F. F. Bruce *JCOONT*, pp. 19–20. Bruce suggests (*ibid*, p. 23) that Tacitus' hostile tone towards Christians indicates that he did not gain his information from them, but from 'some official record', but Wells points out that there is no incompatibility between a hostile attitude and careful cross-questioning of those on trial, as may be seen from the case of Pliny, to which we shall refer below. (Tacitus was governor of Asia at about the same time as Pliny was dealing with Christians in the next-door province of Bithynia, and may well have been obliged to make similar investigations himself.)

I find Wells' argument entirely convincing. Tacitus' reference to 'Christus' is evidence only for what was believed about Christian origins at the time he wrote, and there is plenty of other evidence for that. It is, of course, entirely consistent with what we learn from the New Testament about the execution of Jesus, and to that extent is a positive rather than a negative factor for Christian apologetics. But by itself it cannot prove that events happened as Tacitus had been informed, and certainly it cannot carry alone the weight of the role of 'independent testimony' with which it has often been invested.

Another pagan writing which *may* refer to Jesus as a historical figure (as opposed to merely mentioning his name – for which see the next section) is an obscure letter in the British Museum, which is not so often noticed by writers on the evidence for Jesus.[6] It is in Syriac, and its date is quite uncertain except that it must be later than the destruction of Jerusalem in AD 70 and the subsequent dispersion of the Jews, to which it refers. Its author, Mara bar Serapion, is otherwise unknown. His derogatory references to 'the Jews' suggest that he was not a Jew, and a Christian would hardly have put Jesus (if it *is* Jesus he refers to) on a par with Socrates and Pythagoras, nor would he have talked of his 'living on in the teaching which he had given' (rather than in his resurrection). Mara is, in fact, clearly an adherent of Stoic philosophy, and refers at one point to 'our gods', hardly a Jewish or Christian phrase! He speaks of 'the Jews' as 'executing their wise king' shortly before their kingdom was abolished, but this 'king', unlike Socrates and Pythagoras with whom he is compared, is not named.

This *could* be a pagan reference to the death of Jesus, the 'king of the Jews'. But there are too many uncertainties to allow it much weight as historical evidence. In particular, there is no guarantee that it was written *soon* after AD 70 – it could be a century or more later, since the deaths of Socrates and Pythagoras, which are discussed in parallel with that of the Jewish 'king', were already centuries old (that of Pythagoras being more a matter of legend than of history).[7] If it was much later, there is no more reason to see this writer as independent of Christian tradition than there was for Tacitus. In fact, while not a Christian himself, his attitude to the destruction of Jerusalem as a punishment for the Jews' execution of their 'king' sounds very like an echo of Christian polemic against the Jews.

Early pagan references to the life or death of Jesus then add up to only the most meagre amount of evidence, and that apparently derived from Christian tradition rather than from independent records.

Bruce mentions also, as a possible first-century pagan reference to Jesus, a certain Thallus. None of his work has survived, but a third-century Christian writer, Julius Africanus, refers to him as explaining the darkness at the time of Jesus' crucifixion by an eclipse of the sun. Unfortunately, he does not give Thallus' words, so that we do not know whether Thallus actually mentioned Jesus' crucifixion, or whether this was Africanus' interpretation of a period of darkness which Thallus had not specifically linked with Jesus. In addition, since the date of Thallus' writing is not known, there can be no certainty that, if he *did* refer to Jesus explicitly, this reference may not have been drawn from Christian sources and therefore may be no more independent than that of Tacitus. On Thallus see Bruce, *JCOONT*, pp. 29–30, and the reply by Wells, *Did Jesus Exist?* pp. 12–13.

2. Jewish sources

If we find little or no independent confirmation even of Jesus' existence from pagan writers, are we any better off when we turn to Jewish sources? Wells thinks we are not, but I do not believe that the various references to Jesus by non-Christian Jews can as easily be traced to Christian origins.

(a) Josephus

By far the most important witness is Josephus, whose massive works on Jewish history were compiled towards the end of the first century AD. His *Jewish War*, written shortly after the event, and based to a large extent on his own experience, begins with a sketch of Jewish history from the Maccabaean period, before focusing for the bulk of its seven books on the events of the years AD 66–73. This is not, therefore, such a likely place to look for references to Jesus and in fact there are none. But Josephus' *Antiquities of the Jews* is a more ambitious if less carefully researched work, covering the whole period from the creation to AD 66, and devoting no less than six of its twenty books to the century from the reign of Herod the Great to AD 66. Surely in such a detailed history of the period in which Jesus lived we might reasonably expect to find him mentioned, if he made even a small mark on the history of his people.

And he is mentioned, just twice. By way of comparison we might note that John the Baptist, who was in many ways a similar figure to Jesus, with a popular following which apparently continued for some time as a religious movement after his death,[8] is mentioned only once, at similar length, even though Josephus presents him as a significant figure, of sufficient political importance to be executed as a potential leader of revolt.[9]

The shorter of the two references to Jesus is in *Antiquities* XX 200. In the year AD 62 the newly appointed high priest, Ananus, was speedily deposed because he illegally 'convened the court of the Sanhedrin, and brought before them the brother of Jesus the so-called Messiah, who was called James,

and some other men, whom he accused of having broken the
law, and handed them over to be stoned'.

The men are not described as Christians (Josephus nowhere uses the word except in the passage shortly to be
discussed), but no reason for the high priest's hostility is
mentioned other than James' relationship with Jesus, and the
historicity of James' martyrdom as a Christian leader in AD 62
is generally agreed. This is an important event in the early
history of the church, but as far as our knowledge of Jesus is
concerned, the passage offers little – merely that he had a
brother called James, and that he was known as 'the Messiah'
(*Christos*).

What *is* important for our purpose is the way Josephus
records this title of Jesus in passing, without comment or
explanation. The term *Christos* occurs nowhere else in
Josephus, except in the passage we are shortly to study. This
in itself is remarkable, since we know that messianic ideas,
and the term 'Messiah' itself, were much canvassed in first-
century Judaism; apparently Josephus did not share this
interest. But surely in that case it is highly improbable that he
should refer so casually to Jesus as 'the so-called Messiah'
without explaining for his Gentile readers what this means.
Two explanations are suggested: either Josephus never wrote
these words, and they are a Christian interpolation, or he is
referring back to a previous explanation of this title attributed
to Jesus. In other words, this short reference to Jesus in Book
XX depends on the longer one in Book XVIII. If the longer
one is not genuine, this passage lacks its essential background; if this passage is what Josephus wrote, then the
previous discussion of Jesus cannot easily be dismissed as a
Christian interpolation either.

We shall consider shortly the arguments about the authenticity of the longer passage. It is well known that Josephus'
works were much used by Christians, and owed their survival
to Christian copying, and it is not at all improbable that
Christians should have altered the text to suit their own
needs – in fact it is generally agreed that they did so.[10] But
this bare mention of James, the brother of Jesus, with no

account of his significance in the Christian movement, and no attempt either to deny the charge of law-breaking or to enhance his image in any way, does not look like a Christian interpolation.[11] Still less does the phrase 'the so-called Messiah' (*ho legomenos Christos*), which is hardly the way a Christian would refer to his Lord.[12] And the authenticity of the passage is further supported by the fact that Origen, writing in the first half of the third century, expresses his surprise that Josephus, who did not accept Jesus as the Messiah, nonetheless testified to the innocence of James.[13] This shows that Josephus' text as Origen knew it (a) referred to James the brother of Jesus, (b) mentioned Jesus, and (c) indicated that Josephus himself did not accept Jesus as Messiah. Origen actually quotes from Josephus the phrase *ho legomenos Christos*.[14]

Antiquities XX 200 is, therefore, generally accepted to be what Josephus wrote.[15] It tells us little about Jesus by itself, but the mere fact that it presupposes an earlier explanation of the phrase *ho legomenos Christos* makes it very difficult to eliminate the earlier and longer account of Jesus as a Christian interpolation. To this longer account we now turn. It is known as the *Testimonium Flavianum* ('Flavius' was Josephus' adopted Roman name).

In Book XVIII of the *Antiquities* Josephus relates some of the provocative actions of Pontius Pilatus. Two such anecdotes take up sections 55–62, and Josephus eventually returns to the theme in sections 85–89, where he relates Pilatus' ultimate dismissal. In between these accounts of Pilatus is a series of three apparently unconnected narratives, one about Jesus, the *Testimonium Flavianum* (63–64), one about a scandal in Rome involving the priests of Isis (65–80), and one about a Jewish 'con trick' in Rome which led Tiberius to expel the Jews from the city (81–84). These last two events, which Josephus deliberately brackets together, happened about AD 19, well before the governorship of Pilatus in Judaea, so that it seems this whole section of Book XVIII is a not very carefully compiled collection of miscellaneous events relating to the theme of bad relations between the Jews and Rome. (The Isis scandal did not involve Jews directly, but is introduced as a parallel to the Jewish 'con trick', two incidents which together persuaded Tiberius to take action against eastern religious cults in Rome.) Both the brief account of Jesus and the longer pair of stories about scandals in Rome are introduced by a vague connecting phrase 'And about this time'.

All this makes one wonder how Wells can argue[16] that if the passage about Jesus is removed 'the argument runs on in proper sequence'. To achieve such a 'proper sequence' one would surely need to excise also sections 65–84, so that the Pilatus stories could stand together. Yet these sections relate to events which are independently attested to both by Tacitus and by Suetonius.[17] If then sections 65–84 are accepted as a genuine part of Josephus' account, there can be no structural reason for questioning sections 63–64 either. Indeed, sections 63–64 fit far better here than 65–84, since they do relate to the same historical period, and in fact directly mention Pilatus.

It is in any case typical of Josephus' style to include short stories as 'digressions' in the course of an ongoing narrative, triggered by some aspect of the main story, but not themselves part of its flow. For instance, the account of John the Baptist similarly 'interrupts' the narrative of the wars of Herod Antipas with Aretas.[18]

Any argument against the authenticity of the *Testimonium Flavianum* must therefore be based on its actual content, rather than on its place in Josephus' work. It must also reckon with the fact mentioned above that the reference to Jesus in XX 200 demands an earlier account of him in Josephus' story. And in fact most scholars accept that Josephus' work did contain an account of Jesus at this point. What is disputed is rather how it was originally worded.[19]

In the standard text of Josephus the *Testimonium Flavianum* runs as follows:

About this time there lived Jesus, a wise man, if indeed one should call him a man. For he was a performer of astonishing deeds, a teacher of men who are happy to accept the truth. He won over many Jews, and indeed also many Greeks. He was the

Messiah. In response to a charge presented by the leading men among us, Pilatus condemned him to the cross; but those who had loved him at first did not give up, for he appeared to them on the third day alive again, as the prophets of God had spoken this and thousands of other wonders about him. And still to this day the tribe of Christians, named after him, has not disappeared.

(Antiquities XVIII. 63–64)

For a man who nowhere else shows any interest in either messianic movements in general or Christians in particular, this is remarkable language, and few would want to argue that Josephus wrote just those words. It is widely accepted that the passage has been 'improved' by a Christian editor from Josephus' original wording. But any reconstruction of a more 'likely' wording must be purely conjectural, since there are no significant variations in the manuscripts which survive. It is clear that by the early fourth century at the latest the text as we have it was accepted as genuine, since Eusebius twice quotes it in full, with only very slight variation from the wording of our manuscripts in one of his quotations.[20] We are, therefore, reduced to *assuming* that Josephus could not have written words like 'He was the Messiah', and 'he appeared to them on the third day alive again', and to guessing what original wording might have been doctored to give this Christian version.

Origen could not have known the text in this form, for he concluded from his text of Josephus that Josephus did not accept Jesus as Messiah (see above p. 27). Indeed, without using the word 'Messiah', Josephus elsewhere (*BJ* VI 312-313) argues that the Old Testament promise of a world-ruler to arise out of Judah was in fact fulfilled in the Roman emperor Vespasian, who was promoted from his military command in Judaea to be emperor! It seems that even Christians at a later period found it impossible to believe that Josephus could have written these words about Jesus, for when Jerome (*De Viris Illustribus* 13) quotes this same passage, in a Latin version which is at other points a straight translation of our received text, the clause in question has been altered to 'he *was believed to be* Christ'.

Some of the phrases are typical of Josephus' style (which is
a further indication that the passage was not a wholesale
interpolation by someone else). Thus the description of Jesus
as 'a wise man' is not typically Christian, but is used by
Josephus of e.g. Solomon and Daniel.[21] Similarly, Christians
did not refer to Jesus' miracles as 'astonishing deeds'
(*paradoxa erga*), but exactly the same expression is used by
Josephus of the miracles of Elisha.[22] And the description of
Christians as a 'tribe' (*phylon*) occurs nowhere in early
Christian literature, while Josephus uses the word both for
the Jewish 'race'[23] and for other national[24] or communal
groups.[25]

So the passage is a tantalising mixture of clearly Christian
affirmations with phrases and ideas more typical of Josephus
the detached observer than of Christian propaganda. It is this
which leads many to reconstruct an 'original' version which
was at least non-committal, if not positively hostile to Christianity. Thus the clause 'if indeed one should call him a man'
makes good sense as a Christian response to Josephus' description of Jesus as (merely) a 'wise man', but is hardly the
sort of language a Christian would have used if writing from
scratch. And if, as in XX 200, Josephus had written 'he was
the so-called Messiah' (*ho legomenos Christos*), it would have
been natural for a Christian reviser to leave out *legomenos*.
At the same time, part of what Josephus originally wrote may
have been cut out altogether by the Christian reviser.

All of this means that any reconstruction of Josephus'
account of Jesus will be largely a matter of personal opinion as
to what he is likely to have written. Here is Bruce's proposed
reconstruction, which assumes a hostile rather than neutral
tone in the original text:[26]

Now there arose about this time a source of further trouble[27] in
one Jesus, a wise man who performed surprising works, a teacher
of men who gladly welcome strange things.[28] He led away many
Jews, and also many of the Gentiles. He was the so-called Christ.
When Pilate, acting on information supplied by the chief men
among us, condemned him to the cross, those who had attached

themselves to him at first did not cease to cause trouble, and the tribe of Christians, which has taken this name from him, is not extinct even today.

At any rate, it seems safe to assume that Josephus spoke of Jesus' wisdom and teaching, his wonder-working activity, and his wide following, and that he at least noted the belief of his followers that he was the Messiah, even if he did not also record their belief in his resurrection. At the heart of the account, and the reason for its inclusion at this point in the *Antiquities*, is the record of his crucifixion by order of Pilatus.

This amounts to a substantial testimony to the historical Jesus. But is it independent? Might not even the conjectural 'original' text be itself, like Tacitus' record, merely an account of what Christians were saying at the time Josephus wrote?

This time that explanation will not do. Firstly, the distinctively non-Christian terminology we have noted suggests that Josephus is giving his own account. Secondly, there is no reason whatever for Josephus even to mention Jesus and Christianity at this point in his work at all unless he was convinced that the career and execution of Jesus was an actual event which occurred during the governorship of Pilatus. And thirdly, Josephus, a Jew who lived for much of his life in Palestine, is in a very different situation from Tacitus to know whether what he is told is true or not, and to have an interest in checking what he is told. Nor does the rest of his work encourage us to believe that he was in the habit of talking to Christians or using them as sources of information.

If, then, as I have argued, Josephus did originally include an account of Jesus in his record of the governorship of Pilatus, we have every reason to be confident that he had his own good reasons for believing what he wrote to be true. While it is a pity that we cannot be sure just what he did write, the scepticism which dismisses the *Testimonium Flavianum* wholesale as a Christian fabrication seems to owe more to prejudice than to a realistic historical appraisal of the passage.

There is an interesting different version of the *Testimonium Flavianum* preserved in a tenth-century Christian Arabic work, the history of the world written by Bishop Agapius of Hierapolis. This version omits 'if indeed one should call him a man', and instead of his 'astonishing deeds' and teaching speaks of his good conduct and virtue; Pilatus acts alone, not under Jewish instigation; the resurrection is mentioned only as what his disciples reported; and most significantly 'He was the Messiah' is omitted, but instead the report of the resurrection is followed by 'accordingly he was perhaps the Messiah concerning whom the prophets have recounted wonders'. This is obviously a much less 'committed' version than the received text, and some have suggested that it might be the original. Its attestation is very late, however, and E. Bammel has argued that certain features in its wording point rather to its being a deliberate adaptation of Josephus' account in the light of Christian controversy with Islam (*Ex. T* 85 (1973/4) pp. 145–147). But in so far as this version is not obviously dependent on the received text, it is an important further indication that, as has been argued above, there was an account of Jesus by Josephus underlying the Christianised text which had replaced it by the time of Eusebius. The Agapius text first became widely known with the publication of S. Pines, *An Arabic Version of the Testimonium Flavianum and its Implications* (Jerusalem: Israel Academy of Sciences and Humanities, 1971).

(b) Rabbinic traditions

To search in Rabbinic literature for data on any historical subject is a daunting task. The sheer bulk of the literature, its baffling complexity and (to us) lack of logical structure, its complicated oral and literary history and the consequent uncertainty about the date of the traditions it preserves, all this makes it an uninviting area for most non-Jewish readers. Add to this the fact that history as such is not its concern, so that titbits of 'historical' information occur only as illustrations of abstruse legal and theological arguments, often without enough detail to make it clear what historical situation is in view, and the task seems hopeless. In the case of evidence for Jesus we have the further complicating factor that he was, for the Rabbis, a heretical teacher and sorcerer, whose name could scarcely be used without defilement, with the result that many scholars believe that they referred to him by pseudonyms (e.g. Ben Stada, or Balaam) or by vague expressions like 'so-and-so'. The result of all this is that, in all the vast bulk of Rabbinic writings, very few passages unambiguously refer to Jesus of Nazareth, and those offer us more polemical invective than historical reminiscence.

We would expect any independent information (i.e. not derived from debate with Christians) to come from the early 'Tannaitic' period, that is the period up to the compilation of the Mishnah about AD 200. This restricts our search effectively to four types of sources, the Mishnah itself, the 'Tannaitic Midrashim' (Mekilta, Sifra and Sifre), the Tosefta (a separate compilation of Tannaitic traditions which were not included in the Mishnah), and *baraitoth* (further Tannaitic traditions which were later incorporated in the Talmuds, distinguished as Tannaitic either by the names of the Rabbis cited or by a formula such as 'it is taught', or 'the Rabbis have taught', and preserved in Hebrew rather than in the Aramaic of the later talmudic material). Of these the Mishnah and the Tannaitic Midrashim offer us no relevant material. We shall look therefore at the few passages from the Tosefta or in talmudic *baraitoth* which can most plausibly be seen as referring to Jesus of Nazareth.

Babylonian Talmud Sanhedrin *43a*[29]   This passage is discussing the Mishnah's requirement[30] that, when a man is condemned to death by stoning, even immediately before his execution a final public appeal must be made for any evidence in his favour. In this connection:

It is taught: On Passover Eve they hanged Yeshu.[31] For forty days beforehand a crier went out proclaiming, 'He is going out to be stoned, because he has practised magic and led Israel astray. If anyone has anything to say in his defence, let him come and speak for him.'[32] But they found nothing in his favour, so they hanged him on Passover Eve.

It is generally agreed that 'Yeshu' is Jesus of Nazareth (he is so referred to in other talmudic passages, and one manuscript

of the Talmud adds the words 'the Nazarene' here) and the
death on Passover eve[33] rings true. Beyond that there is little
resemblance to the gospel accounts, and in particular the
forty-day period of public appeal is generally seen more as an
apologetic device (Jesus was given every chance to prove his
innocence) than as a historical reminiscence (the Mishnah
knows no such lengthy appeal procedure).[34] Two factors are
significant, however. Firstly, while the reference to 'hanging'
may well be a reminiscence of the crucifixion (or at least an
acknowledgement that this was how Christians believed Jesus
to have died), the context is entirely that of a *Jewish* punishment appropriate to a blasphemer, with no reference to the
involvement of Rome. Secondly, the specific charge is a
distinctively Jewish one, 'magic and leading Israel astray'. It is
these charges which will continue to recur in later Jewish
polemic, but they were already there in the gospel accounts
(see e.g. Mark 3:22; Matthew 9:34; 10:25 for the charge of
sorcery, and Matthew 27:63 for the description of Jesus as
'deceiver' (*planos*), a term which suggests the Jewish *mesith*,
one who entices others into idolatry).

> The *baraita* is followed by a response from the third-century
> Rabbi Ulla to the effect that while Jesus certainly could not be
> defended against the charge, the problem in his case was that he
> was 'close to the kingdom'. This intriguing phrase has been
> variously interpreted. Does it mean that he had influential con-
> nections in the government, and might this be an obscure remi-
> niscence of Pilatus' reluctance to convict? Or does it reflect the
> Christians' claim that Jesus was of Davidic (and therefore royal)
> descent? We simply do not know what Ulla was referring to, and
> in any case his comment is surely too late to have independent
> value as evidence.

A further *baraita* referring to Jesus follows immediately,
brought in here no doubt primarily because Jesus' execution
has just been mentioned, though it is not entirely irrelevant
since it too talks about the execution of 'heretics'. It begins:
'Our Rabbis have taught: Yeshu had five disciples – Matthai,
Neqai, Netzer, Buni and Thodah.' It then goes on to describe

how each of these five was condemned to death. The whole story is a series of elaborate puns on the five names. With the exception of Matthai, none of the names can with any plausibility be linked with those known from the gospels and Christian tradition, and the function of the names is not to record historical data but to provide a basis for the word-game which follows. The passage *may* indicate a reminiscence that Jesus was known to have had a close circle of disciples, and that one of them was called Matthew, and it again links Jesus with the theme of judicial condemnation. The unusual number of the disciples and the widely different names suggest that the passage does not derive from Christian information, but it can hardly be taken seriously as historical evidence.

Babylonian Talmud Sanhedrin *107b*[35]   The context is a discussion in the Mishnah[36] of Old Testament characters who have no place in the world to come. One is Gehazi, whom Elisha, it is stated, repulsed with both hands; similarly 'Rabbi Joshua ben Peraḥiah repulsed Jesus (the Nazarene) with both hands'. This then leads into the following story:

> When King Jannaeus was killing our Rabbis, Rabbi Joshua ben Peraḥiah (and Jesus) escaped to Alexandria in Egypt. When peace was restored, Simeon ben Sheṭaḥ sent him a message: 'From me, the holy city (Jerusalem), to you, Alexandria in Egypt (my sister). My husband is living in you, and I am deserted.' So he set off, and came to a certain inn, where he was given a warm welcome. He said, 'How lovely is this *aksania*!'[37] He (Jesus) replied, 'Rabbi, she has narrow eyes.' 'You scoundrel,' said R. Joshua, 'is that what you are thinking about?' So he sounded four hundred trumpets, and excommunicated him. Many times Jesus came and pleaded to be allowed back, but he would not listen. But one day, when R. Joshua was reciting the Shema, Jesus came to him, and he decided to welcome him back, and made a gesture to him. Jesus, however, thought he was ordering him away, and he went and set up a brick and worshipped it. R. Joshua then appealed to him to repent, but he replied, 'I have learned from you that no chance of repentance is allowed to one who sins and leads others into sin.' And a teacher has said, 'Jesus the Nazarene practised magic and led Israel astray.'

This bizarre story serves well to illustrate the problem of searching in Rabbinic literature for historical data! The misunderstanding about the innkeeper may not be as trivial as it sounds, since there *may* be a theological disagreement about Jerusalem involved cryptically under the figure of an inn,[38] but no satisfactory origin has been suggested for the absurd idea of worshipping a brick. And the historical setting is impossible, since Joshua ben Peraḥiah lived a century before Jesus.[39]

The importance of the passage lies not in historical data, but in the insight it gives us into an early Jewish view of Jesus, as a heretic and sorcerer who led Israel astray – but one who only gradually degenerated into this after being a disciple of a respected Rabbi.[40] In addition it is an early example of the frequently repeated Rabbinic assertion that Jesus had associations with Egypt (even though this is not here, as in other passages, given as the explanation for his knowledge of magical arts).[41] But for historical evidence on the life of Jesus, this confused story seems to have nothing to offer.

Tosefta Hullin *2:22–24*[42]   The subject under discussion is the danger of defilement by having anything to do with a *min* (heretic, a term particularly used for Christians, but also more generally applied). Two illustrative stories are given, the first of which concerns Rabbi Ishmael, who died about AD 135: 'Rabbi Eleazar ben Dama was bitten by a snake. And Jacob of Kefar Sama came to heal him in the name of Jesus ben Pantera. And Rabbi Ishmael did not allow him.' Eleazar disputed the decision, but died before he could argue his case, whereupon Ishmael congratulated him on dying without 'breaking down the hedge erected by sages'.

The second story is about Rabbi Eliezer ben Hyrcanus, who flourished at the end of the first century AD. He was accused of *minut* ('heresy'), and, though acquitted, was puzzled as to how the charge had arisen. His pupil Akiba suggested that he might have heard something from a *min* and been pleased by it. He replied: 'By Heaven! You remind me. Once I was strolling in the camp of Sepphoris. I bumped into Jacob of Kefar Sikhnin and he told me a teaching of *minut* in the name of Jesus ben Pantiri, and it pleased me.'[43]

These stories confirm what we know from other sources, that by the end of the first century the followers of Jesus were clearly identified as heretical by the Rabbinic establishment. Neither of the Jacobs mentioned can be identified. As far as evidence about Jesus himself is concerned, the stories indicate that healing and teaching were the activities associated with his followers (and therefore presumably with him), and that he was referred to as Jesus ben Pantera (the name occurs in various related forms).

The name Pantera is associated with Jesus in several Rabbinic passages, and Origen[44] confirms that Jewish anti-Christian polemic in the second century spoke of Jesus as the son of Mary born as a result of adultery with 'some soldier called Panthera'. While it is perhaps fanciful to claim that this name was coined as a corruption of the Greek *parthenos*, 'virgin', it is possible that this slur was the Jewish response to the Christian story of the virgin birth. This would, however, provide evidence only for what Christians were saying about Jesus by the end of the first century, not for any independent knowledge of an unusual parentage.

A tombstone discovered at Bingerbrück in Germany, and apparently dating from the first century AD, is that of an archer called Tiberius Julius Abdes Pantera, from Sidon. He belonged to a cohort which apparently served in 'Syria' before being transferred to the Rhine in the year AD 9. While the stone proves that the name Pantera was known at the time, it is the most remarkable flight of fancy to suggest that this man was in fact Jesus' father; so Morton Smith, *Jesus the Magician* (London: Gollancz, 1978) p. 47, faithfully followed by D. Stewart, *The Foreigner* (London: Hamish Hamilton, 1981) p. 17, and by the writer of the photograph caption in I. Wilson, *Jesus – the Evidence* (London: Weidenfeld and Nicolson, 1984) p. 63. Wilson himself (*ibid*, p. 64) is more circumspect! 'Syria' is a large area, and there is no evidence to link this man with Galilee or Judaea.

We have noted that some believe 'Ben Stada' to be a Rabbinic pseudonym for Jesus, though the issue is hotly debated. The main reason for this identification is a passage in

the uncensored version of Babylonian Talmud, *Sanhedrin*
67a.[45] It is stated that in convicting a *mesith* (one who entices
others into idolatry) it is permissible to use the testimony of
hidden eavesdroppers:

> This is what they did to Ben Stada in Lydda, and they hanged him
> on Passover Eve. Ben Stada was Ben Pandira. R. Ḥisda said,
> 'The husband was Stada, but Pandira was the lover.' But the
> husband was Pappos ben Judah – it was the mother who was
> called Stada. Yet the mother was actually called Miriam, a
> women's hairdresser – but in Pumbeditha we say, This woman
> has been false to (*s'tath da*, presumably a pun on the name Stada)
> her husband.

Various factors suggest a connection with Rabbinic accounts
of Jesus: the fact that Ben Stada is presented as a *mesith*, the
hanging on Passover eve (cf. *Sanhedrin* 43a above), the
similarity of Ben Pandira to Ben Pantera, the mother's name
Miriam (= Mary), and the accusation of her adultery. In the
Rabbinic discussion of who is who it seems likely that 'Ben
Stada' is being interpreted to mean 'Son of an adulteress', but
there were clearly differing views about Ben Stada's identity
and parentage, which this debate is designed to reconcile. The
location of the execution in Lydda is a problem for the
identification with Jesus, as is the mention of Pappos ben
Judah, who lived a century after Jesus. So while it is not
unlikely that later Rabbis identified Ben Stada with Jesus, we
should be very cautious of assuming that any Ben Stada
tradition originated as a historical reminiscence of Jesus.[46]

These few Rabbinic passages about Jesus (and there are no
others which clearly refer to him from the Tannaitic period)[47]
must suffice to give something of the flavour of the anti-
Christian polemic which continued to grow in Jewish literature until in the late middle ages quite substantial *Toledoth
Yeshu* (lives of Jesus) were in circulation, giving vivid details
of his supposedly adulterous origin, his practice of magic, and
his flagrantly sacrilegious behaviour and apostasy.[48]

What is the value of all this as historical evidence? Very
little, one must admit, in the light of the confusion of dates,

people and circumstances which characterises the Rabbinic stories, and the bizarre character of much of their contents. But it seems clear that by at least the early second century Jesus was known and abominated as a wonder-worker and teacher who had gained a large following and had been duly executed as 'one who led Israel astray'. Uncomplimentary as it is, this is at least, in a distorted way, evidence for the impact Jesus' miracles and teaching made. The conclusion that it is entirely dependent on Christian claims, and that 'Jews in the second century adopted uncritically the Christian assumption that he had really lived'[49] is surely only dictated by a dogmatic scepticism. Such polemic, often using 'facts' quite distinct from what Christians believed, is hardly likely to have arisen within less than a century around a non-existent figure.

B. INDIRECT EVIDENCE

So far we have looked at non-Christian sources which may be claimed to tell us something about Jesus himself as a historical figure. Now we turn to other non-Christian passages which mention Jesus not so much as a historical figure but rather as an object of worship. This section deals, then, more with evidence for early Christianity. Clearly this is at best indirect evidence for Jesus himself; that there were in the first century people called 'Christians' who owed allegiance to someone called 'Jesus' or 'Christ' does not by itself necessarily tell us anything about that person, or even demand that he actually existed, any more than the existence of Buddhists tells us much about the historical existence of Gautama, the Buddha. And yet there is a difference, for the sources we are talking about relate to a period within a century of the lifetime of Jesus, and it is at least the most economical explanation of such references to believe that they deal with a historical figure whose life and teaching were such as to give rise within a generation or two to an enthusiastic following which was to develop into a major religion. As general corroboration, therefore, for the Christians' own account of

their origins in the life of Jesus these passages are not irrelevant, even though their force is indirect.

1. Gentile writers

We have already mentioned Tacitus' account of the persecution of the Christians in Rome in AD 64, and have seen that his
report indicates a group of followers of 'Christus' in Rome at
this time which was large enough to form a suitable scapegoat
for Nero, and distinctive enough to have incurred already a
large measure of unpopularity. (Indeed in the sentence immediately following the passage quoted earlier Tacitus suggests that they were convicted not so much for arson – the
ostensible charge – but *odio humani generis*, 'for hatred of
the human race', which could mean either the Christians'
supposedly anti-social tendencies or the hatred which the
human race as a whole felt towards them; either way it is clear
that Christians were generally unpopular, quite apart from
Tacitus' own prejudice against this and other similar 'deadly
cults'.)

Two other Roman writers contemporary with Tacitus mention the followers of 'Christus'. Suetonius, who published his
Lives of the Caesars about AD 120, also includes a reference to
Nero's action against Christians, of whom clearly Suetonius
has no higher opinion than Tacitus. In the course of a list of
abuses corrected by Nero the following tantalisingly brief
sentence occurs: 'Punishments were inflicted on Christians, a
class of men belonging to a new and vicious cult' (Suetonius,
Nero 16.2). We are given no indication of what they were
punished for, nor in what their 'wrongdoing' (*maleficus*,
translated 'vicious' above) consisted. The great fire of AD 64 is
not mentioned in this connection, and indeed the punishment
of Christians is included in that part of the book (up to section
19) which deals with Nero's *good* acts, before he turned to
vice and crime. (The fire is not reported until section 38,
where it is unconditionally blamed on Nero himself.) Nor
does Suetonius even so much as mention the 'Christus' from
whom their name derived.

But such a mention has often been claimed in another passage, not this time about Christians, but about Jews. In recounting Claudius' attitudes to other races, Suetonius mentions an event which is normally dated in AD 49 (and which is mentioned also in Acts 18:2): 'He expelled the Jews from Rome, because they were constantly rioting at the instigation of Chrestus' (Suetonius, *Claudius* 25.4). Again absolutely no further details are given. Communal riots involving Jews were not an uncommon occurrence in the Graeco-Roman world, and perhaps needed no explanation. But who is Chrestus, and why is he mentioned?

The simplest explanation is surely that he was a person otherwise unknown to history, who had somehow achieved a position of influence in the Jewish community at Rome (about whose internal affairs at this period very little is known). Chrestus (a Greek word for 'good' or 'kind') was apparently a common enough name, especially of slaves. But two facts have been taken to suggest a different explanation.

First, Chrestus is a *Greek* name. Of course many Jews did have Greek names, whether from birth or assumed later (e.g. Jesus' Galilean disciples Andrew and Philip, and all seven of the 'deacons' appointed in Acts 6:5, only one of whom is said to be a proselyte), but Chrestus is not otherwise known as a Jewish name.[50]

And secondly Chrestus would sound very like Christus, which, with its meaning 'anointed', would be unfamiliar in the Gentile world, so that a substitution of the familiar Greek name Chrestus would be easily made. Indeed Tertullian points out that the opponents of Christianity, by mispronouncing the name as 'Chrestianus', in fact testified to its 'sweetness and kindness'![51]

Is this, then, a mistake by Suetonius who, having heard that a certain 'Christus' was responsible for the riots (i.e. that they were between Christian and non-Christian Jews?), firstly wrongly assumed that 'Christus' was there at the time and secondly substituted the more familiar name Chrestus? Perhaps (and this surmise has been hallowed by frequent repetition), but it can never be more than a guess, and the fact that Suetonius can elsewhere speak of 'Christians' as members of a new cult (without any reference to Jews) surely makes it rather unlikely that he could make such a mistake. That there were Christian Jews at Rome in AD 49, as Acts 18:2 indicates, is likely enough, but that Suetonius made any reference to them, let alone to their founder, in connection with Claudius' decree is improbable. In that case, we simply do not know who 'Chrestus' was.[52]

From Suetonius then, we can deduce with confidence only what we already know from Tacitus, that a group known as Christians, who were thought to be a nuisance, existed in Rome during the reign of Nero. He tells us nothing about Jesus himself.

The other contemporary of Tacitus who refers to Christians is Pliny the Younger, who was governor of Bithynia for two or three years about AD 110. From Bithynia he wrote numerous letters to Trajan about the administration of the province, one of which concerns the problem of how to deal with Christians. This cultured and pedantic administrator assumes that Christians should be tried and punished as such, but is not sure what legal precedents have been established. His practice has been to give them an opportunity to renounce their Christianity, but if they persist he has executed them, unless they were Roman citizens, in which case they were sent to Rome for trial. Many who were accused of being Christians have been persuaded to invoke the (pagan) gods, to make an offering to the emperor's statue, and to 'curse Christ', 'none of which, I am told, genuine Christians can be forced to do'. Others, under interrogation, had told him what their alleged 'guilt or error' consisted of:

> They were in the habit of meeting before dawn on a fixed day, when they would recite in turn a hymn to Christ as to a god, and would bind themselves by oath, not for any criminal act but rather that they would not commit any theft, robbery or adultery, nor betray any trust nor refuse to restore a deposit on demand. This done, they would disperse, and then they would meet again later to eat together (but the food was quite ordinary and harmless).[53]

This was all Pliny could discover, and he concludes that it was 'a perverse religious cult, carried to extremes'. He apologises for troubling the emperor about it, but it is affecting large numbers of all classes, and needs to be checked.[54]

Trajan's reply curtly approves of Pliny's action, prefers to let sleeping dogs lie, but agrees that those convicted of being Christians and unwilling to recant must be punished. (He gives no help to Pliny on the nature of the punishment, which is what the letter was about in the first place!)

This correspondence is clearly of the first importance for assessing both the numerical strength and the practices of the Christians in Asia Minor at the beginning of the second century, and for the insight it gives into the way educated Romans thought about this 'contagious superstition'. But for our purposes, looking for evidence about *Jesus*, it has nothing specific to offer. He is clearly by now an object of worship and of personal allegiance even at the cost of martyrdom, but Pliny seems to have discovered nothing about him as a historical figure; even the name 'Jesus' does not appear at all in the letters.

2. Jewish writers

Our study of the Jesus traditions in the Rabbinic literature has indicated that Jewish leaders of the Tannaitic period were well aware of Christians as a distinct group, the disciples of Yeshu. As such they shared the opprobrium attached to Jesus himself as a sorcerer, blasphemer and heretic. References to *minim* are thought frequently to have Christians particularly in view. But in all this there is nothing of historical substance to add to the meagre 'direct' evidence we have already collected.

But if Rabbinic writings are not the most likely type of literature to provide historical evidence about early Christianity, surely in Josephus we should be on firmer ground. Would it be possible to write a detailed history of the Jews up to AD 66 (the *Antiquities*) and an even more detailed account, largely first-hand, of the war of AD 66–73 (the *Jewish War*) without referring from time to time to the new and growing sect within Judaism which was coming to be called 'Christian'? Yet that is precisely what Josephus did. The word 'Christian' occurs only once in his writings, in the mention of the 'tribe of Christians' deriving its origins from Jesus, which we considered above (*Antiquities* XVIII 64). The only other recognisable reference to Christians is the account, also considered above, of the execution of a number of men including James, the brother of Jesus the so-called Christ, on a charge of breaking the law (*Antiquities* XX 200), and even there, when speaking of the acknowledged leader of the Christian church in Jerusalem, Josephus manages to avoid either the name 'Christian' or any indication that it was as members of this group that they were killed.

And yet we know that there *were* plenty of Christians around both during the period Josephus wrote about and at the time of his writing. Is not this fact significant for any argument from silence in this area? Those who suspect the historicity of the Jesus of the gospels on the grounds that there are so few early non-Christian references to him, must surely, by the same argument, be even more sceptical as to whether the Christian church existed in the first century. But not even George Wells wishes to deny this! As has so often been noted, absence of evidence is not evidence of absence.

Perhaps it may help to get this fact in perspective if we suggest a modern parallel. It is hard to travel much around Britain today without becoming aware of the existence of the Church of Jesus Christ of Latter-day Saints, or the 'Mormons'. They knock on doors, distribute literature, and are building churches all over the country. By any standard they are an impressive social and religious phenomenon. But how much do Mormons, and their founder Joseph Smith, figure in the work of most British writers today? How many historical studies written today mention them? Even in specifically religious writing, I would guess that references to Mormons do not bulk largely except in two types of writing – either by Mormons or specifically against them. If only a tiny proportion of our literature survives to the year 4000 (and no newspapers), how much non-Mormon evidence will there be for twentieth-century Mormonism, or for the life of Joseph Smith?

Is not this roughly the position of Christianity in first-century Palestine? However strong it may have been 'on the ground', and however important it may appear from its own writings, is it likely that among the few pieces of non-Christian literature surviving we would find more reference to Christians, and to Jesus, than we do in fact find?

As Christianity grew and gained influence, and ultimately achieved political power, the situation changed. If Mormonism were to meet with similar success, it would no doubt also figure more prominently in the writings of secular historians. But when that happened, the historians of the day would find themselves obliged to turn largely to Mormon sources in piecing together an account of Mormon origins. So it is too for Christianity. Surely here there is little cause either for Christian embarrassment or for historical scepticism. It is what you would expect.

C. BACKGROUND EVIDENCE

From the meagre results of our search so far for non-Christian evidence for Jesus, one might well wonder what is the basis of the claim often heard today that new discoveries are constantly enriching, and changing, our knowledge of the Jesus of history. None of the material we have considered is at all newly discovered. So what are these new discoveries which have purportedly so changed our understanding of Jesus?

They fall mainly into two categories. Firstly, there are some relatively new discoveries not in the area of non-Christian evidence, but in that of Christian or semi-Christian (especially Gnostic) writings of the period after the New Testament. To this material we shall turn in the next chapter.

But secondly, the most exciting and fruitful area of expanding knowledge with relation to Jesus consists not of any reference, direct or indirect, to Jesus himself in non-Christian sources, but of what we might call circumstantial evidence, a richly enlarged awareness of the sort of world in which he lived, and the sort of people he might have mixed with. If we are to see Jesus as his contemporaries saw him, we need to know the way they thought, and the sort of stereotypes against which they might have tried to measure him. And this is what is becoming increasingly possible, even if there are still large and tantalising areas of uncertainty. It is this sort of circumstantial evidence rather than any new 'biodata' on Jesus himself which has formed the main basis for the many new estimates of Jesus we hear today.

Some of our increasing knowledge of Jesus' environment derives from brand-new discoveries, of which by far the most celebrated and important are the Dead Sea Scrolls, dug up from 1947 onwards. But much of it is not so much new discovery as a new willingness of Christian scholars to look at non-Christian material which had long been available, to draw out of Rabbinic writings, classical literature, papyri, inscriptions and other such sources material which helps to reconstruct the world Jesus lived in. Today a new emphasis on the sociological aspect of the study of ancient history is leading to a more realistic understanding of what life was really like. If all this tells us nothing about Jesus himself, it does enable us to interpret what we already know about him more realistically, as we see him as a real man of his times, and try to put ourselves in the shoes of those who first encountered him in Galilee and Jerusalem.

At this point we shall look briefly at the nature of this 'background evidence'. In the final chapter we shall return to consider in broad outline how it may affect our understanding of Jesus.

This is now such a vast area of study that a full survey would be quite out of proportion. Instead I will offer a few soundings which I hope will together give a representative impression of the sort of evidence available and the way it may be used to fill out our picture of Jesus.

1. Qumran[55]

'The greatest manuscript find of modern times'; 'without precedent in the history of modern archaeology'; 'this fabulous documentary and archaeological material'; 'a revolution in our understanding of Christian origins'. Such language coming from sober scholars gives some indication of the impact of the discovery since 1947 of a dozen ancient scrolls in Hebrew and Aramaic, together with the fragmentary remains of hundreds more, in caves near the north-west corner of the Dead Sea, and the subsequent excavation of the headquarters of the community to which they belonged, Khirbet Qumran. The community has turned out to be an ultra-orthodox Jewish group, which deliberately set up its headquarters in the wilderness to keep itself separate from the 'apostate' Jewish establishment in Jerusalem. Living by a strict monastic code, they devoted themselves to the systematic study of the scriptures and of later religious texts, in preparation for the coming great day when God would lead them, the 'Sons of Light', to final victory over all the 'Sons of Darkness'.

The sect began its separate existence just before the middle of the second century BC, and survived until the Roman invasion of AD 66–73. Most scholars agree that they were Essenes, a group referred to by Josephus and other writers, but about whom not very much was previously known.

All very interesting – but what has this to do with Jesus and Christian origins? In the early days many wild claims were made of direct links between Jesus and the Qumran sect, even including the theory that it was itself a Jewish Christian sect, and that its founder, the mysterious 'Teacher of Righteousness', was Jesus himself.[56] Others, noting similarities between some expressions and ideas in the Qumran writings and those of some New Testament writers, notably John, have suggested that all the 'distinctive' ideas of Christianity were in fact derived from Qumran, the Christian movement being a deviant form of Essenism.[57]

In the euphoria of a new discovery such extreme conclusions were understandable, if not excusable. Nowadays saner assessments have prevailed, and it is accepted that direct links between Jesus and this remote sect are very unlikely. The nearest approach which can be suggested with some plausibility is that John the Baptist, in the context of whose

preaching Jesus' mission was launched, may have had some
links with the sect during his period of revivalist preaching
in the 'wilderness' by the Jordan[58] – but if so they were not
apparently very influential, for John's message and his activity are more clearly distinct from those of Qumran than
they resemble them.

No, the importance of the Qumran discoveries for the
history of Christianity is as what I have called 'background
evidence'. Our knowledge of first-century Judaism has been
significantly expanded. Before 1947 virtually no documentary
material of the inter-testamental and early Christian periods
had been discovered in Palestine. We had, of course, various
post-biblical Jewish works (the so-called Apocrypha and
Pseudepigrapha), as well as the literary works of people like
Josephus, but all these were preserved in later copies, whose
authenticity was sometimes suspect; but now a new source of
information, whose authenticity cannot seriously be doubted,
has opened up a whole area of Jewish life which was previously unknown, and the period it covers is precisely the period
leading up to and including the lifetime of Jesus. If Judaism
had previously been understood largely in terms of the 'mainstream' groups, especially the Sadducees and the Pharisees,
the Qumran texts have made abundantly clear what was
already partially understood from the Pseudepigrapha, that
not all Jews belonged to this 'main-stream'.

And if there was one such group of which, but for the
accident of a goat-herd's discovery, we might still have been
in complete ignorance, were there not perhaps more such,
whose documents still await discovery, or were left in places
whose climate is less kind to leather and papyrus than the dry
caves of Qumran?

At any rate, if there was ever a temptation to think of
'first-century Judaism' as a uniform social and religious
phenomenon, that is no longer possible, and this is an important factor in our understanding of the impact of Jesus, the
'unorthodox' religious teacher, on the Jewish public. And
where there are significant similarities in language between
the Qumran texts and the New Testament, while direct

'borrowing' is highly unlikely, we may be able to appreciate better how Jesus and his followers took words and ideas that were familiar in the religious world of their day, and used and adapted them to express their own new message (which, surely it hardly needs to be said, is in itself fundamentally different from the legalistic, 'monastic' and apocalyptic outlook of the Essene sect).

Because this one sect has recently come so dramatically to light it is easy to exaggerate its importance in its own times. To us, it is the most important Jewish group outside the mainstream, simply because it is the only one of which we are well informed. But this is no guarantee that a Jew of that time would have regarded it as any more influential than a similarly separatist cult would be likely to be today. Scholars have sometimes been guilty of trying to explain everything in the light of Qumran, just because that light is now available to us.

But without going to that extreme, it is certainly true that the discovery of Qumran has filled in an important part of the wider background to Jesus' life and teaching.

2. Galilee

If Qumran was both geographically and socially remote from the main area of Jesus' life and ministry, what can be said about the area where he grew up and where the bulk of his recorded activity took place?

Until fairly recently it was common not only among non-specialists but also among historians and New Testament specialists to speak of 'Palestine' and of 'Palestinian Judaism' as if this were somehow a monochrome unity, and to assume that what could be said of Palestine was *ipso facto* as true of Galilee as it was of Judaea. In recent years, however, there has been an increasing interest in the study of Galilee in its own right, and it has become clear that it was a province with a very different history, population, culture and outlook from the southern part of Palestine.[59] Cut off from Judaea by the hostile territory of Samaria, and surrounded on other sides by pagan populations, 'Galilee of the Gentiles' was a place apart.

Not that there is any evidence of a desire to sever links with Judaea. The temple at Jerusalem, as long as it was standing, was the focus of Galilean religious and patriotic loyalty, and Galilean pilgrims to the annual festivals at Jerusalem came south in large numbers. The aim of those zealot-type leaders who arose in Galilee was the independence of the Jews, not of Galilee. But nonetheless Galilee was different, and its separate system of government under Herod Antipas accentuated the difference.

Later Rabbinic writings (which come from the Pharisaic wing of Judaism) give the impression that Galilee was lax in matters of the law. The truth may be rather that the more conservative and essentially rural population of Galilee had never accepted the Pharisaic system which became dominant after the destruction of the temple, but which was already influential in Jerusalem in the time of Jesus, and which seems to be the teaching of the 'scribes and Pharisees' which we find in confrontation with Jesus in the gospels. It is possible, then, that behind Jesus' disagreements with the Jewish leaders over matters of legal observance there lies not only his personal authority to interpret the will of God but also an already existing conflict between the religious traditions of different parts of the country.

Certainly there were strong social and cultural differences. While no part of Palestine was free of the influence of Hellenism by the time of Jesus, Galilee had been more strongly and consistently exposed to it. It seems clear that Greek was widely spoken in Galilee, even though Aramaic remained the vernacular (and 'Mishnaic' Hebrew was also in use, perhaps in more formal contexts), so that Jesus the Galilean would be likely to be at least bilingual.[60] It seems clear too that the Galilean form of Aramaic was significantly different from that of Judaea, so that a Galilean accent would be obvious in Jerusalem, and probably would attract some not altogether good-humoured comment. In fact later Rabbis clearly despised Galileans as uncultured and even boorish, and it is likely that this feeling was not unknown even at the time of Jesus.

All this and much more has been noticed not so much by the discovery of new documents and archaeological finds but by the careful study of literature which had long been available, but which yielded new insights when read in the light of suggested regional variations. While there is much here that remains uncertain, it can hardly now be doubted that Jesus, as a Galilean in Jerusalem, was not among his own people, culturally speaking, that he might well have had social or class barriers to overcome, and that his debates with Judaean Pharisees took place against a background of an already existing suspicion of any religious teaching which came out of Galilee. An awareness of these factors can throw useful light on our understanding of several aspects of the accounts of Jesus' ministry.

3. Holy Men

If Jesus was famous as a miracle-worker and teacher, were there any existing categories into which such a character might be fitted, at least superficially? What do we know of such 'holy men' in the first century?

The pagan world of the eastern Mediterranean had long been familiar with them. An early example was Pythagoras, who lived in the late sixth century BC. Essentially he was a philosopher who founded an important philosophical school, but to his later followers he was more a miracle-working holy man than an academic; it came to be believed that he 'possessed miraculous knowledge, had power over animals, commanded winds and waves, could transport himself over great distances in an instant, banished an epidemic and performed cures by means of music and song'.[61] From such beginnings the image of the miracle-working 'divine man' developed to the point where many influential figures, statesmen, philosophers, teachers, were credited with supernatural powers, particularly in healing. Even the very down-to-earth emperor Vespasian (who is said to have joked on his deathbed about his 'becoming a god')[62] is credited with healing a blind man and a cripple when he was on a visit to Alexandria – it was

expected of him as emperor, and though he himself doubted
that he had any such power, the cures were duly performed.[63]
Theissen[64] has argued that such beliefs, and the stories that go
with them, enjoyed a particular vogue in the first century AD,
with 'the rise of a new irrationalism'.

The best-known pagan example of this type at the time of
Jesus is the Neo-Pythagorean sage, Apollonius of Tyana, who
apparently lived through most of the first century AD, and
whose life was told at tedious length by a third-century
admirer, Philostratus.[65] He was, according to Philostratus, an
itinerant teacher of morals and philosophy, a reformer of
religious cults, whose ascetic life was modelled on the traditions of Pythagoras, and who was put on trial by both Nero
and Domitian for his opposition to their tyranny. He was
credited with numerous miracles and displays of supernatural
knowledge; healings and exorcisms feature prominently, including the raising from the funeral bier of a girl apparently
dead. Several of the stories bear an interesting resemblance to
those in the gospels, and it is possible that Philostratus was
influenced by some knowledge of Christian claims about
Jesus when he compiled his work; but there is no reason to
doubt that the figure of Apollonius as he emerges from the
book would have fitted comfortably into the pattern of
popular thinking in the eastern Mediterranean at the time of
Jesus.

Judaism too had its miracle-working holy men, in the
tradition of Moses, Elijah and Elisha. Around the time of
Jesus two such holy men stand out, men whom Vermes has
labelled 'charismatics' to distinguish their less rule-bound and
even unorthodox piety from that of the more traditional
Rabbis. The various traditions about Honi the Circle-Drawer
(first century BC) and Hanina ben Dosa (first century AD) are
conveniently brought together in Vermes' *Jesus the Jew.*[66]
Hanina is the better-known of the two, apparently a younger
contemporary of Jesus, and also a Galilean, a man of poverty,
piety, and supernatural powers rather than a teacher and
debater on matters of legal observance. It was Hanina's very
distinctness from the normal image of the Rabbi which made

him remarkable, but the existence of at least two such 'char-ismatics' around the same period as Jesus is surely a signifi-cant factor in estimating how the ordinary Galilean might have reacted to Jesus' unorthodox behaviour and teaching.

In Judaism, as in the wider world at that time, demon possession was a matter of common concern, and exorcism a regular and valued ministry, as indeed Jesus himself pointed out (Matthew 12:27). Ḥanina ben Dosa was credited with power over the queen of the demons, and other Jewish exorcists outside the Christian circle are referred to in the New Testament (Mark 9:38; Acts 19:13–14), and in Josephus.[67] Here too is a background of existing practice against which Jesus' exorcisms would need to be understood.

Again in the recognition of the tradition of miracle-working holy men we are not dealing with new discoveries, but with the synthesis of existing information into a clearer picture of the world Jesus lived in, information which was in some cases until recently familiar only to specialists outside the area of New Testament studies. It is through such contributions to our historical perspective that we may expect to gain a more realistic understanding of Jesus in his own context.

4. Freedom fighters

1973 saw the commemoration of the nineteenth centenary of the Roman conquest of Masada, and the publicity given to that event brought a new public awareness of (and sympathy for) the 'Zealots', those uncompromising loyalists whose implacable opposition to Roman rule led ultimately to the destruction of Jerusalem and its temple, and to their own mass suicide as the Roman siege-works were completed.

It is clear that the revolutionary outlook represented by these men was an important factor in first-century Palestine. It first broke out in AD 6 when the Romans held a census to form the basis for the taxation of Judaea, newly brought under direct Roman rule after many years under Herod and his son Archelaus. Judas 'the Galilean' raised an armed revolt on the grounds that the people of God should not be slaves to a pagan power. The revolt was soon put down, but it became the inspiration for subsequent risings, most of which were efficiently nipped in the bud, culminating in the great revolt of AD 66.

It has become customary to refer to all these freedom fighters as Zealots. But in fact there is still much debate as to the proper application of this term, and it is likely that it was not in fact used as a 'party' name before AD 66. Anyone of this viewpoint could, however, appropriately be called a 'zealot' for Israel's national and religious interests; cf. Paul's use of the term in Galatians 1:14; also Acts 21:20; 22:3. Simon 'the Zealot' mentioned in Luke 6:15 and Acts 1:13, need be no more than a zealot in Paul's sense, not necessarily an advocate of armed revolt. Before AD 66 the term we find more frequently is Sicarii (dagger-men), and it was this group which apparently had the most fierce reputation for guerilla activities. During the war of AD 66–73 the Sicarii and the Zealots were rival factions (there were others too), and the heroic defenders of Masada were in fact Sicarii, not Zealots, according to Josephus.[68] Among these extremists the family of Judas the Galilean continued to hold a prominent place, including Menahem, the leader of the revolt in Jerusalem in the early part of the war, and Eleazar, the leader of the last stand at Masada.

Jesus (the Galilean!) could no more ignore the existence of this movement than a black public figure in South Africa today can avoid taking a stand with relation to the ANC. What stand he took has been much debated, some arguing that he was in agreement with the 'Zealot' approach, and that it is only the whitewashing activities of the gospel writers which have obscured the fact from us,[69] others more plausibly interpreting his message as a more radical alternative to Zealot politics, focusing on the kingdom of God rather than the kingdom of Israel.[70] But what we cannot do is imagine a Jesus who operated in a purely pietistic world antiseptically isolated from the violent currents of Jewish nationalism deriving from Judas the Galilean and his like. Their passionate longing for the independence of Israel, and their willingness to take violent action to achieve it, is an essential part of the background against which a 'real' Jesus must be understood.

5. The 'man in the street'

One of the problems of history, especially of ancient history, is that it depends largely on books, and therefore on the views and interests of the sort of people who write books. From the literature that has survived we can learn a lot about the priests, the politicians, the Pharisees whose traditions formed the Mishnah, even the learned 'monks' of Qumran. But most Jews were neither Pharisees nor Sadducees, had no political influence, did not write religious treatises and could not have read them either. How did they think? What were the hopes and fears and daily concerns which made up their lives? The question is important for us, because it was, apparently, the 'common people' who formed the bulk of Jesus' following – indeed it was from among them that Jesus himself and his inner circle of disciples came. It is such people who form the most immediately relevant 'background' to Jesus' ministry.

In Luke 2:25–38 we meet two otherwise unknown people, Simeon and Anna. Both are devout worshippers, but neither apparently holds any official position in the temple. Are they representative, then, of the ordinary pious Jew? We simply do not know, but what is striking about them is their expectation of an imminent work of God, the 'consolation of Israel' (Luke 2:25). There is absolutely no reason to see them as sympathisers with later 'Zealot' tendencies (Judas the Galilean had not yet raised the standard of revolt), but perhaps this phrase picks up a popular current of expectation which was to lead people naturally to discuss Jesus in 'messianic' terms.

Old Testament messianism had developed over the intervening centuries in various directions, often independently, but a growing voice in the literature that has been preserved from the period is that of the 'apocalyptic' movement. The men of Qumran, with their expectation of a coming final battle between good and evil, when God himself would come to fight against the forces of darkness, were one example of this trend. Outside the walls of Qumran it is likely that it often took on a more earthy, nationalistic tone; what the Zealots wanted to achieve for themselves by force of arms, the apocalyptists prayed and believed would be achieved for them by God's cataclysmic intervention, when the whole evil world-order would be transformed into the messianic kingdom of the people of God. Until then, they must wait in hope – it would not be long.

There seems no reason to doubt what the gospels plainly indicate, that some such expectation (even if not embellished with all the more fanciful elements of the apocalyptic scheme) was very much alive in the ordinary 'Jew-in-the-street', whether in Galilee or Judaea. What is less clear is how strongly such a belief would have been in his consciousness in his day-to-day living. It does not seem likely that the Galilean peasantry, for all their basically religious cast of mind, would have differed very much from country people everywhere and at all times, in that they would have been more concerned from day to day with the price of grain than with the exact definition of sabbath restrictions, and with provisions for the coming winter than with the date of the coming kingdom of God.

In other words, in assessing the background to Jesus' ministry, we must beware of the assumption which our limited historical sources might seem to suggest, that everyone he met was a Pharisee, a Sadducee, an Essene, or a Zealot (any more than it would be fair to divide up present-day Britain without remainder into committed supporters of the main political parties).

6. Background evidence and the distinctiveness of Jesus

These few soundings into the social and religious history of the world Jesus lived in (and they are only a few samples from what is now a vast area of historical reconstruction) are intended to show that, even where Jesus himself is not mentioned, non-Christian sources offer us a wealth of vital information on the sort of situation in which he must have found himself, the sort of people he would have mixed with, and the sort of categories within which his contemporaries would be likely to try to understand him. This is an indispensable part of 'the evidence for Jesus', once it is granted that he lived at all in first-century Palestine. It is only against the background of such knowledge that we can hope to understand what the gospels tell us about him in the appropriate historical context, rather than imposing on them the foreign categories of our modern European stereotypes. Such evidence may enable us sometimes profitably to 'read between the lines' of the gospels (provided that we heed C. S. Lewis' warning that in so doing we do not fail also to read the lines themselves!).[71] Some of the results of this reading will be outlined in our final chapter.

But there are potential dangers in this approach, in two opposite directions. On the one hand, some Christians feel threatened by the discovery that Jesus was not the only healer and exorcist around, and that some of the cures attributed to Apollonius and Ḥanina bear a striking resemblance to those recorded in the gospels, or that some of the language familiar to us from the New Testament is not unlike that of the Qumran texts. In reaction, they tend to play down the areas of similarity as much as possible, and to emphasise the distinctiveness and superiority of Jesus to such an extent that he becomes less and less credible as a real man of his times.

On the other hand, for some the discovery of these areas of similarity is an invitation to question whether Jesus was really distinctive at all, and to make of him just one among the many aspiring Zealot leaders, or charismatic Rabbis, or apocalyptic visionaries, or wandering magicians, according to the preference of the interpreter. To discover a 'parallel' to Jesus in the contemporary world is, for this school of thought, to 'explain' Jesus and his teaching, as derived from and reflecting what was already the common currency of his day.

In response to this latter approach, the Jewish scholar Samuel Sandmel gave a stimulating lecture under the title 'Parallelomania',[72] in which he insisted that Christianity was 'a Jewish movement which was in particular ways distinctive from other Judaisms'. He went on, 'Only by such a supposition of such distinctiveness can I account to myself for the origin and growth of Christianity and its ultimate separation from Judaism. If, on the other hand, the particular content of early Christianity is contained in and anticipated chronologically by the Dead Sea Scrolls and anachronistically by the rabbinic literature, then I am at loss to understand the movement . . . I am not prepared to believe that the writers of Christian literature only copied sources and never did anything original and creative.'[73] It was a salutary warning, which has not always been heeded in recent studies of Christian origins.

We need, then, to avoid these two extremes. 'Background' evidence must remain in the background, and must not be allowed to dictate the shape of the picture which emerges from the primary evidence of the gospels. Sometimes it will illuminate the nature of Jesus' ministry more by contrast than by assimilation. We must be prepared to discover in Jesus 'the man who fits no formula',[74] and who transcends and challenges the patterns of first-century life and thought at crucial points.

But provided that Sandmel's caution is observed, there is nothing to be frightened of in the recognition of points at which Jesus fits into the world of his day as we are able to reconstruct it. Rather this is, as we shall see later, a cause for excitement, as it opens up the possibility of seeing Jesus 'in the round', rather than as the cardboard cut-out figure of a merely theological abstraction.

Chapter
2

Christian Evidence Outside the New Testament

Non-Christian evidence may tell us much about the world in which Jesus lived, but we have found that it can offer us little firm data about Jesus himself beyond the fact of his existence as a figure of history, and the most rudimentary indications of the nature of his life and death. For anything more than this we are, for better or worse, dependent on what his followers have preserved of their memories and interpretation of the historical origins of their faith.

For most modern readers to speak of the earliest Christian sources is to speak of the New Testament. All, or very nearly all,[1] the Christian writings of the first century that have been preserved are in the New Testament, and it is there that we might reasonably expect to find the best-informed historical records of Jesus. But it is not impossible that other records of Jesus might have been preserved within the Christian churches, and, though not surviving in use in the church in the way the New Testament books have, might still come to light in quotations by later Christian writers who read these records, before they were lost, or who had received them by oral tradition. And then there is always the archaeologist's dream, that ancient copies of such long-lost writings might actually be uncovered, preserved in the dry sands of Egypt. If the documents of the Qumran sect could be preserved from the first century, may there not be Christian documents of a similar age to be discovered?

Before we turn to the New Testament, then, we need to examine what information about Jesus may be derived from such sources.

A. THE NATURE OF THE EVIDENCE

Early Christian writers do in fact quite frequently quote traditions of Jesus which are not found in the New Testament. Sometimes they name the source from which they are quoting; often they simply give a 'saying of the Lord' which is otherwise unknown. The majority of this material consists of sayings rather than new stories about Jesus, and we shall look at a selection of such sayings shortly.

But in addition the archaeologist's dream has been increasingly fulfilled during the last century, as undeniably ancient documents have come to light, some of them as old as our oldest copies of the New Testament books themselves. Many are only isolated fragments, but some are whole documents purporting to record stories, or more often sayings, of Jesus.

A few examples may serve to indicate the nature of the material.

Egerton Papyrus 2   One of the oldest fragments may be seen on public display in the British Museum. The manuscript has been confidently dated to the second century. It consists of three small fragments of a papyrus document, less than thirty square inches in all, which formed part of a collection of Egyptian papyri purchased by the British Museum in 1934. It contains parts of a number of stories and discourses of Jesus which are recognisably similar to some in the canonical gospels, but are different in detail, and in a few cases quite unknown. We shall note one of these independent stories later.[2]

Oxyrhynchus Papyri 1, 654, 655   Excavations in the years 1897–1907 at the site of the ancient city of Oxyrhynchus, near the west bank of the Nile, uncovered a rich hoard of ancient papyrus documents, publication of which is still continuing eighty years later. Among the most notable were three fragmentary texts, written in the second and third centuries, which contained Greek sayings attributed to Jesus, most of which were not known at all from the canonical gospels, while the rest were significantly different in form and wording.

These sixteen isolated sayings[3] caused great excitement – here was apparently new material from the Jesus-traditions which had been preserved outside the canonical gospels. How it was preserved was not known until the discovery of the Nag Hammadi library (see next section), which included a full text in Coptic of the Gospel of Thomas, a collection of sayings of Jesus to which we shall return. The first seven sayings in the Gospel of Thomas are recognisably the same as those in Oxyrhynchus Papyrus 654, and in the same order, and those in the other two papyri also reappear in the Gospel of Thomas, in each case in the same order. It seems clear then that these papyri represent extracts from a Greek original underlying the Coptic Gospel of Thomas.

The Nag Hammadi Library   Further up the Nile, near the village of Nag Hammadi, some Egyptian peasants in 1946 came across a large jar containing thirteen ancient papyrus books. These add up to a total of around a thousand large pages, most of which are in reasonably good condition, so that this find is on a far larger scale than most of the collections of papyrus fragments previously discovered. Each book contained several complete works, a total of about fifty. They are in Coptic (the ancient Egyptian language, written in Greek letters), and were written not later than the second half of the fourth century AD, though the origin of the writings is in most cases much earlier than the time they were copied. Many of them were certainly written as early as the second century. In character they vary widely, some being clearly pagan (including even an extract from Plato's *Republic*!), others Jewish, but many are clearly Christian, and some purport to record the sayings of Jesus. We shall look more fully at their character below.[4]

These three finds are mentioned here only as examples of the sort of recent discovery which has offered the hope of new material to fill out the portrait of Jesus and his teaching which the canonical gospels offer. There have been many other such finds. We shall notice more below in discussing the Gospel of Peter and the 'Secret Gospel of Mark'.

It is now clear that there were by the end of the second

century many writings purporting to give an account of Jesus, and the flow continued for a long time after that.[5] A few were fairly similar in form to the New Testament gospels, but most focused more on Jesus' teaching than on his acts, and many consisted entirely of sayings alleged to come from him. While some of them contained material found also in the New Testament gospels, in most cases it occurred in a much expanded or altered form, and a great deal of the material had no canonical parallel.

Some of these writings have been preserved for us virtually intact, but most exist only in fragmentary form or have disappeared altogether. Several are known by name because they are referred to by early Christian writers who may quote sayings or incidents from them, but any attempt to reconstruct what they may have been like is very hazardous. For instance we read in patristic writings of a Gospel according to the Hebrews, a Gospel of the Nazaraeans, and a Gospel of the Ebionites, but scholars are far from agreed whether these were separate works, or different names for one or two Jewish-Christian gospels.[6] Each 'quotation' may be treated on its merits, but it has to be interpreted, unfortunately, without its original context.

The one feature which quickly becomes obvious as one reads what remains of these apocryphal 'gospels' is that a high proportion of them are clearly angled towards a Gnostic interpretation of Jesus' life and teaching. This is true, for instance, of all the 'Christian' material from Nag Hammadi, which clearly represents the library of a Gnostic group. And much that is not Gnostic is equally clearly designed to promote other doctrinal tendencies which are known to have developed in second-century and later Christianity, such as the doctrine of the 'harrowing of hell' or the perpetual virginity of Mary.

'Gnosticism' is a broad term for a tendency in religious/philosophical thought in the early Christian period which affected various religious traditions, including Christianity. Gnostic Christians were clearly very numerous, especially in Egypt where, owing to its dry climate, most of the ancient documents with which we are concerned have been found. What became 'orthodox' Christianity clearly had to fight hard to resist Gnosticism, and the writings of such church fathers as Irenaeus are full of attacks on Gnostic ideas. The discovery of these documents from the Gnostics themselves has shown that he did not exaggerate the fundamental divide between Gnosticism and orthodoxy.

Gnosticism must have been an approach which appealed primarily to the intellectual – perhaps that is why it eventually failed to establish itself more widely. Perhaps its nearest equivalent today would be such cults as Theosophy or Rosicrucianism, which combine some Christian language and themes with other mystical and philosophical elements, and which emphasise the need for initiation into the higher realms of 'truth' in order to experience true enlightenment and 'salvation'. Such cults have always appealed to the religious dilettante, but they are also capable of inspiring devoted commitment, fostered by the sense of belonging to an esoteric brotherhood on a level above that of the ordinary man.

The Gnostic view of the world was dualistic. Matter is evil, and the created world, including the human body, is a prison from which the soul longs to escape into spiritual freedom. But this world is under the influence of the surrounding spheres, a graduated series of 'heavens', each progressively further removed from the world. To be saved is to be set free by true enlightenment, and so to ascend to the higher realms of the spirit, into the company of the vast hierarchy of non-earthly beings who inhabit the different heavenly spheres. Into such a scheme Jesus can be fitted not as a true incarnation of God – such an idea would be quite abhorrent – but as a divine saviour who penetrates through to earth and, appearing in human form, can offer true knowledge to those who welcome his teaching. They are set free by this knowledge (*gnosis*), and so can leave the evils of earth behind.

It follows from such a view of Jesus that his life and death on earth, if they are noticed at all, can be little more than an unfortunate necessity; what matters is his teaching. And the Gnostic writings which have been preserved reflect this emphasis. The so-called 'Gnostic Gospels'[7] contain hardly any narrative, and are essentially philosophical or mystical treatises on the Gnostic understanding of the world and of the heavenly realms, designed to convey true saving *gnosis*. Sometimes there is no narrative setting at all, the word 'gospel' being used in the sense of a saving message rather that to indicate a literary category parallel to that of Matthew, Mark, Luke and John.[8] Where there is a narrative setting, and the teaching is presented as the words of Jesus, this is most commonly in the form of a purported address by Jesus to his disciples after his resurrection.[9] Thus the Sophia of Jesus Christ begins as follows:

> After he rose from the dead, his twelve disciples and seven women followed him and went to Galilee onto the mountain that is called 'Place of Harvest-time and Joy'. When they gathered together, they were perplexed about the origin of the universe, the plan, the holy providence, the power of the authorities, and concerning everything that the Saviour does with them in the secret of the holy plan. The Saviour appeared not in his first form, but in the invisible spirit. And his form was like a great angel of light . . . And he said 'Peace to you! My peace I give to you!' And they all wondered and were afraid. The Saviour laughed and said to them, 'What are you thinking about? Why are you perplexed? What are you searching for?' Philip said 'For the origin of the universe and the plan'. The Saviour said to them, 'I desire that you know . . .'[10]

Thereafter the remainder of the work consists of a lengthy Gnostic treatise on the invisible world beyond and its inhabitants, a treatise which in part corresponds closely to a non-Christian Gnostic work, the letter of Eugnostos the Blessed, also found at Nag Hammadi. In this case it seems, therefore, that a pagan Gnostic treatise has been taken over by Christian Gnostics, and given a Christian narrative setting as a discourse of the risen Jesus.

There is, therefore, little to be expected by way of historical information about Jesus from such writings; that is not their area of interest. It is theoretically more likely that they might have preserved some of the teaching of Jesus, and in the case of the Gospel of Thomas this has been argued with some force, as we shall see. But a little reading around among the Nag Hammadi documents will soon make it clear what a totally different world of thought they belong to from that of the Jesus we know from the New Testament. And in view of the undeniable tendency of such writings to put into Jesus' mouth teaching which derives from non-Christian Gnosticism, or to adapt elements of his teaching known from the New Testament in patently Gnostic directions, it is hard to see how such genuineness might be established other than by a purely subjective impression.

It is in fact on such subjective grounds that certain non-canonical sayings and incidents have been picked out by some scholars as possibly preserving genuine memories of the historical Jesus. We shall look in what follows at a few such cases, both sayings and stories, which have been preserved with little indication of their source or original context. Then we shall go on to take some samples of more complete works of the second century which, if they do not give us much plausible evidence about the historical Jesus, will serve to give a taste of the way the traditions about him were developing within not much more than a century of his death.[11]

B. A SELECTION FROM THE EVIDENCE

1. Some uncanonical 'sayings of Jesus'

Interest in, and knowledge of, the so-called *Agrapha* (Greek for 'unwritten things') was stimulated especially by a book of J. Jeremias entitled *Unknown Sayings of Jesus*.[12] Jeremias collected alleged sayings of Jesus from any source outside the canonical gospels, including the rest of the New Testament (see next chapter), early Christian writers, papyrus documents such as we have been discussing, and even an Arabic inscription over the gateway of an early seventeenth-century mosque in India![13]

Among other interesting sayings (many of which are clearly Gnostic or in other ways reflect second-century developments

of thought) Jeremias isolates twenty-one 'whose attestation
and subject-matter do not give rise to objections of weight,
which are perfectly compatible with the genuine teaching of
our Lord, and which have as high a claim to authenticity as the
sayings recorded in our four Gospels'.[14]

It will be obvious that this statement bristles with questions:
What is an 'objection of weight'? Who decides? How is
compatibility with 'the genuine teaching' measured? What is
a 'high claim to authenticity'? In the end it seems that the
dominant criterion is the modern scholar's estimate of
whether the saying represents the sort of thing the Jesus we
know from the canonical gospels 'might have said' – and this
means that the possibility of any significantly new information
about Jesus' teaching coming from these *agrapha* is rather
remote!

A few examples will illustrate the nature of this material.

Work on the sabbath   In the gospel of Luke according to
the fifth-century manuscript Codex Bezae, between the story
of Jesus' disciples plucking corn on the sabbath and that of his
healing on the sabbath (and in place of Luke 6:5, which is
transferred to follow the latter story), there occurs this brief
episode: 'On the same day Jesus saw a man working on the
sabbath, and said to him, "Man, if you know what you are
doing, you are blessed; but if you do not know, you are cursed
and an offender against the law." '

The radical approach to sabbath-keeping implied here is
certainly similar to other sayings of Jesus. It cannot, of
course, be seriously argued that it was originally a part of the
gospel of Luke (it occurs in *no* other manuscript), but it is not
impossible that the writer of Codex Bezae has here incorporated an independently preserved tradition of a genuine
saying of Jesus. On the other hand, it is equally possible that
such a pronouncement might have been coined at some later
stage of church discussion over sabbath-keeping, and then
fitted with a minimal narrative context. Who is to say?[15]

Temptation   Tertullian,[16] writing at the end of the second
century, quotes Jesus' words, 'Watch and pray, that you may
not enter into temptation', and says that they were preceded

by another saying: 'No one will reach the kingdoms of heaven without being tempted.' Again it is entirely plausible that Jesus might have said some such words in Gethsemane, in order to prepare his disciples for the coming ordeal. The plural 'kingdoms of heaven' (*regna coelestia*) would be unique in a saying of Jesus, though might reflect only a difference of idiom in the process of translation into Latin. How such a saying might have come to Tertullian independently of the canonical gospels can only be guessed.

Ask great things   Clement of Alexandria[17] gives the following as a saying of Jesus: 'Ask for the great things, and the little things will be added to you.' Origen[18] quotes the same words, and then goes on to add a closely balancing verse: 'And ask for the heavenly things, and the earthly things will be added to you.' This last verse is very close to Matthew 6:33, and it is possible that Clement's verse too is simply a later adaptation of Matthew 6:33, whose form it echoes, including the prominent verb 'will be added'. But it goes on being quoted by other early Christian writers as either a saying of Jesus or a text of scripture. Might it then be an independent saying of Jesus? Its theme is clearly consistent with Matthew 6:33, and the direct command to 'ask', with a promise of results, echoes Matthew 7:7. Jesus *could* have said this, but *did* he, or was it a later Christian's paraphrase? Again, who can say?

Christians as money-changers   By far the most frequently-quoted 'saying of Jesus' outside the canonical gospels[19] is a brief and tantalising epigram: 'Be approved money-changers.' It occurs in many early Christian and Gnostic writings, cited sometimes as a saying of Jesus, sometimes as a text of scripture, or as coming from 'the Gospel'.[20] A money-changer has to be able to recognise true and counterfeit coinage, and must not put bad coinage into circulation, so that an 'approved' money-changer is one who is competent in recognising true and false coinage, and responsible in his handling of it. The point of the metaphor is therefore clear enough, and is drawn out explicitly by Origen[21] who interprets this 'command of Jesus' by quoting Paul's injunction in

1 Thessalonians 5:21, 'Test everything; hold fast what is good'.
Jesus often used such comparisons from daily life to illustrate
his teaching (fishers of men, faithful and wise stewards, etc.),
and this saying would fit the pattern. The call to careful
discrimination would reinforce sayings like Matthew 7:6;
10:16, etc. If Jesus did not say something like this, it is not easy
to see how the epigram could have been so widely accepted
and valued as a saying of Jesus from the later second century
onwards.

These are a few examples out of a number of sayings found
in early Christian tradition which may quite plausibly be
attributed to Jesus, and there is no *a priori* reason for doubt-
ing that some of his sayings could have been thus preserved
outside the canonical gospels.[22] They do not add up to a very
impressive body of teaching, and add little that is new or
surprising, for the simple (if circular) reason that anything
which *is* out of keeping with the familiar canonical teaching of
Jesus is thereby automatically suspect as a later coinage
falsely attributed to Jesus. There seems to be no objective
way of avoiding this circularity, and the result is that the study
of *agrapha*, fascinating as it is, is never likely to offer any
serious modification of our knowledge of Jesus, except for
those who are already disposed on other grounds to question
the authenticity of the canonical portrait, and who are therefore glad to welcome alleged sayings of Jesus which support
an alternative interpretation.

2. Some uncanonical stories of Jesus' ministry

As well as the sayings discussed in the last section, there are
some, though comparatively very few, stories of Jesus' ministry similarly quoted or preserved in fragmentary documents.
Some are adaptations or expansions of canonical narratives,
others quite independent. Again just a few examples may be
mentioned

The rich man   The familiar story of the rich man whom
Jesus told to sell all his possessions receives an interesting new
twist in a version attributed to 'The Gospel according to the

Hebrews', and quoted in the Latin version of Origen's commentary on Matthew.[23] Apparently there were two rich men in this version; the second of them, on hearing Jesus' demand 'began to scratch his head, and it did not please him'.

And the Lord said to him: 'How can you say, I have obeyed the law and the prophets? For it is written in the law, You shall love your neighbour as yourself – and see, many of your brothers, who are sons of Abraham, are covered in filth, dying of hunger, while your house is full of many good things, and yet nothing at all comes out of it for them.'

Then follows the familiar saying that it is easier for a camel to go through the eye of a needle than for a rich man to enter the kingdom of heaven.

Sadly we do not know what happened with the first rich man in this version. But what we have here is a slightly embellished telling of the canonical story (the scratching of the head is surely due to a story-teller's licence rather than to historical memory), expanded by a moving ethical explanation of why Jesus made his unwelcome demand. The focus of the story has shifted from allegiance to Jesus to humanitarian concern, and the wording perhaps recalls the parable of the rich man and Lazarus. It seems more likely then, that this version represents a later reworking of the story in the context of Christian ethical instruction, rather than an independent early account of the event.[24]

An encounter in the temple   A single leaf of parchment from a tiny 'pocket edition' of stories of Jesus, probably written in the fourth century AD, was found at Oxyrhynchus in 1905 (Oxyrhynchus 'Papyrus' 840).[25] It contains an account of a visit by Jesus and his disciples to the temple, where they meet 'a certain Pharisee, a chief priest called Levi'. He rebukes Jesus for coming into this holy place and looking at the sacred vessels without having first bathed and changed his clothes, nor have his disciples washed their feet. In response to Jesus' challenge whether he himself is clean, Levi protests that he has indeed been down to the Pool of David and has carried out all the correct ablution ritual.

The Saviour replied, 'Woe to you blind men who cannot see! You have bathed in this poured-out water in which dogs and pigs wallow night and day, and you have washed and rubbed your outer skin – which prostitutes and flute-girls also anoint and bathe and rub and beautify in order to excite men, while inside they are full of scorpions and all wickedness. But I and my disciples, whom you accuse of not having been immersed, have been immersed in living water . . .'

Here the text breaks off, but the point of the story is clear; it is the contrast, so familiar from passages like Mark 7:1–23, between outward cleansing (which may be for quite unholy motives!) and inward purity. The language is harsh, but hardly any harsher than some of the canonical attacks on religious hypocrisy. It is certainly not impossible that such an encounter could have taken place, and that Jesus would react in this way to such a challenge. Some features in the narrative are questionable ('chief priests' were not normally Pharisees, and the purification rituals do not seem to correspond to what is otherwise attested), but Jeremias[26] is able to find explanations for all of them. Even if the story has been written up in the context of later Christianity (when e.g. the description of Jesus as 'the Saviour' would be more normal), and (*pace* Jeremias) with a rather inaccurate knowledge of the temple and its ways, there is no reason why it may not preserve a tradition of an actual incident and dialogue.

A miracle by the Jordan? Among the fragments of Egerton Papyrus 2, mentioned above, is a badly damaged account of what looks like an otherwise unknown miracle of Jesus. The surviving words may be reconstructed roughly as follows:

But when they were perplexed by his strange question, Jesus as he walked stood still on the bank of the River Jordan, stretched out his right hand . . . and sowed on the . . . and then . . . water . . . and . . . before them produced fruit . . . much . . . to the (joy?) . . .

The text is too uncertain to allow more than a hopeful guess, but this may well have been an account of a nature miracle involving the instantaneous growth and fruiting of some plant. Without knowing the context and the sequel it is impossible to say whether this was comparable with the miracles of Jesus as we know them from the canonical gospels, or whether it was more the sort of meaningless display of supernatural power which easily came to be attributed to a man of God in apocryphal writings.

The meeting with James   We know from 1 Corinthians 15:7 that the risen Jesus 'appeared to James' but that is all that the New Testament tells us of the encounter which was apparently the point at which Jesus' sceptical brother changed course, to become eventually the head of the church in Jerusalem. But Jerome,[27] apparently following Origen, gives a fuller version of the incident, which he attributes to the 'Gospel according to the Hebrews':

> But the Lord, when he had given the linen cloth to the servant of the priest, went to James and appeared to him. For James had sworn that he would not eat bread from that time when he had drunk the Lord's cup until he saw him rising from among those who sleep . . .
>   'Bring a table and bread' said the Lord. He took bread, blessed and broke it, and gave it to James the Just, and said to him, 'My brother, eat your bread, for the Son of Man has risen from among those who sleep.'

In view of the subsequent prominence of James among the Jewish Christians, it is not surprising that a Jewish-Christian gospel should feel the need to fill out Paul's bare statement. In the process James has apparently already become a disciple before Jesus' death, and one who was present at the Last Supper. The introduction of an unknown 'servant of the priest' as apparently the first witness of the resurrection is also a new development. Altogether this seems clearly to be a legendary expansion of a detail in the New Testament, and this perhaps gives us a glimpse into the character of what we might have expected to find if the whole of this 'Gospel according to the Hebrews' had been preserved.

I hope this varied selection of uncanonical sayings and stories will suffice to show the sort of 'evidence' about Jesus which is available to us in the fragments of early Christian 'gospels' which have survived either in quotations by patristic writers or on scraps of ancient documents. We turn now to a number of more substantial documents which will significantly fill out the picture.

3. Stories of Jesus' birth and childhood

We have noted that the tendency of second-century Christian literature was to focus on, and to amplify, the teaching of Jesus rather than stories about him. But one prominent exception to this pattern is the fascination which clearly developed from an early date with the events surrounding his birth and childhood. Just as the Christmas stories are probably better known and loved today than other aspects of Jesus' life (and are still subject to sentimental or legendary embellishment), so the early Christians seem to have felt the need for more information about Jesus as a baby and as a child than the canonical gospels offered. Partly this was due to the sheer fascination of the idea of a human child who was also divine – how would such a being behave? What would it have been like to grow up with him? But also the growing veneration of Mary, leading quite soon to the idea that she was herself born sinless, and that she remained for ever virgin, led to a great elaboration of the events leading up to and surrounding Jesus' birth.

Underlying the considerable number of later 'infancy gospels' are two works which were both probably written in the latter part of the second century, and which formed the basis around which further legendary material developed.

(a) The Protevangelium of James[28]
This was a widely popular book, preserved in several languages, despite its ultimate official suppression in the western

church. Many of its contents have been prominent in subsequent art, Christmas carols, etc. Its main subject is not Jesus, but Mary his mother. It tells how she was born in answer to prayer to a childless couple, Joachim and Anna, and was dedicated to God; the story is closely modelled on that of the birth of Samuel. Brought up in the temple until the age of twelve, she was then entrusted (in response to a miraculous sign) to Joseph, an old man who already had a family. There is a long account of the confusion arising from the discovery of Mary's pregnancy, but both Mary and Joseph are ultimately acquitted of having 'stolen marriage'. Then the birth of Jesus in a cave is narrated, primarily through the experiences of the midwife. Great care is taken to establish that Mary's virginity was not broken in the birth of Jesus any more than in his conception. Then we have the story of the wise men, and Herod's attempted massacre, from which the baby John the Baptist is miraculously delivered, though his father Zechariah is murdered at the altar (to be replaced as priest by Simeon).

The birth stories of Matthew and Luke are the essential framework for the later part of this work, incidental details no less than the main stories being worked on to produce a story which both caters for the curiosity of those who found the canonical stories too brief, and also serves to answer some questions they might have raised (e.g. what was the relationship of Joseph with Mary? How could Jesus have 'brothers'? etc.). Above all the book is a product of the movement to present Mary as a worthy object of worship, and to provide her with a 'biography' of her own. It contains several miracles and examples of divine guidance, but it is not nearly so extravagant as most later material which developed from it, much of which is by comparison in rather bad taste.

(b) The Infancy Gospel of Thomas[29]
This curious work has probably no link with the Coptic 'Gospel of Thomas' which we shall consider next. It too has been preserved in various languages and versions, and it was clearly widely influential especially in the eastern

church, from which some of its contents became known to Muhammad, and incorporated in the Qur'an. It deals not with Jesus' birth, but with the unknown period of his childhood up to the age of twelve, concluding with the incident of Luke 2:42–51. Apart from this one story, the rest of the book has no basis in canonical traditions, but consists of an imaginative portrait of what a divine child might be like. The theme is tackled with gusto, if not always with much delicacy. The result is a docetic Jesus, an alien visitor who makes life both uncomfortable and dangerous for those about him, much like the children in John Wyndham's *The Midwich Cuckoos*!

In addition to the well-known story with which it begins, of Jesus making birds of clay on the sabbath, and then clapping his hands to make them fly away, we read of his cursing the son of Annas who spoiled his game, so that he withered up, and of his cursing a boy who bumped into him, whereupon the boy died on the spot, while those who remonstrated with him were struck blind. In the end Joseph is moved to say to Mary, 'Do not let him go outside the door, for all those who provoke him die'! Other miracles are not so destructive, carrying water home in his garment when his pitcher was broken, a miraculous yield of corn, solving Joseph's carpentry problem by stretching wood to fit. Several involve instantaneous healing, including a number of dead or dying friends.

The other main interest is in Jesus' superior wisdom and knowledge, which regularly confounds his teachers, one of whom concludes from Jesus' allegorical explanation of the meaning of the letter Alpha, 'This child is not earthborn'. The pupil becomes the teacher and everyone marvels.

This last aspect perhaps suggests a Gnostic interest in Jesus as the esoteric teacher, but most of the work is not so much promoting a particular theology as simply enjoying a good story. Here lies the main contrast with the infancy stories of Matthew and Luke, which are primarily theological accounts of who Jesus is and of the significance of his coming in the developing purpose of God. The later infancy gospels represent not additional historical information about Jesus, but pious (or sometimes rather secular!) imagination filling in the gap left by the canonical writers' relative lack of interest in story-telling for its own sake.

4. The Gospel of Thomas

We have referred above to the 'Oxyrhynchus sayings of Jesus' and to the discovery of the full text of the gospel from which they came at Nag Hammadi.[30] This Gospel of Thomas consists of a collection of 114 'sayings', many roughly the equivalent of one biblical verse, though the longest are parables of perhaps a dozen verses. They are introduced as follows: 'These are the secret words which the living Jesus spoke, and which Didymus Judas Thomas wrote.'[31]

The introduction suggests a typical Gnostic discourse by the risen Jesus to a disciple such as we have considered above.[32] But the 'narrative' setting is minimal, and the collection which follows is not a connected discourse, but a very varied anthology. About a quarter of the sayings, mostly very short ones, are virtually identical with those known to us from the canonical gospels. Others are obviously connected with canonical sayings, either using their terminology to make a different point, or developing them into new forms. Many of the synoptic parables are here, mostly in rather abbreviated form, but with distinctive features which often significantly affect the application of the parable. But along with his relatively familiar material is a great deal which immediately jars on the ears of anyone who knows the canonical gospels, not only because its terminology is new, but because it reflects different values, which are clearly those of Gnosticism. A selection of sayings may illustrate the point:

2. Jesus said: He who seeks must not stop seeking until he finds; and when he finds, he will be bewildered; and if he is bewildered, he will marvel, and will be king over the All.

19. Jesus said: Blessed is he who was before he became. If you become my disciples and hear my words, these stones will minister to you. For you have five trees in Paradise; they do not move in summer or in winter, and their leaves do not fall off. He who will know them will not taste death.

59. Jesus said: Look upon the Living One as long as you live, that you may not die and seek to see him and be unable to see.
67. Jesus said: He who knows the All but fails to know himself has missed everything.
70. Jesus said: When you beget in yourselves him whom you have, he will save you. If you do not have him within yourselves, he whom you do not have within yourselves will kill you.
77. Jesus said: I am the light which is over everything. I am the All; the All came forth from me and the All has reached to me. Split the wood; I am there. Lift up the stone, and you will find me there.
82. Jesus said: He who is near me is near the fire, and he who is far from me is far from the kingdom.
87. Jesus said: Wretched is the body that depends on a body, and wretched is the soul that depends on both.
108. Jesus said: He who drinks from my mouth will become as I am, and I myself will become he. And the things that are hidden shall be revealed to him.
114. Simon Peter said to them: Let Mary go away from us, for women are not worthy of life. Jesus said: Lo, I shall lead her, so that I may make her a male, that she too may become a living spirit, resembling you males. For every woman who makes herself a male will enter the kingdom of heaven.

This concluding saying is not likely to endear the Gospel of Thomas to modern female readers, even if the chauvinism attributed to Jesus is slightly less extreme than that of Peter! The undesirability of women is a common Gnostic theme, since women are associated with childbirth, and so with the bodily life from which Gnosticism seeks to be emancipated. Clement of Alexandria (*Strom.* III 6) 'quotes' the following exchange 'When Salome asked, "How long will death have power?" the Lord answered, "So long as you women bear children."' In this connection Clement also quotes (*Strom.* III 9) from the 'Gospel of the Egyptians' an alleged saying of Jesus, 'I am come to undo the works of the female', which he interprets by saying that 'the female' means lust and 'the works' are birth and decay!

Most of this is foreign territory for those who are at home in the New Testament gospels, but is familiar ground to those who are acquainted with Gnosticism, and the presence of this gospel among the Nag Hammadi Gnostic texts is not surprising. But a few of these sayings were also current in more orthodox circles. For instance, Clement of Alexandria twice quotes no. 2 above, attributing it to the Gospel according to the Hebrews,[33] while no. 82 above was known to Origen,[34] though he was unsure whether it was a genuine dominical saying or not. It is interesting that Jeremias, writing before the publication of the Gospel of Thomas, and so unaware of the source from which Origen may have derived the saying, was prepared to argue for this as a genuine saying of Jesus independently preserved.[35]

Is it then possible that, despite the clearly Gnostic tendency of much of its contents, this early collection (most would agree that it was compiled about AD 150, at least in its earliest form) has preserved some otherwise lost teaching of Jesus? No blanket verdict can safely be given, but each saying should be examined on its merits. In some cases, particularly in the simpler versions of some of the parables, scholars have argued that this gospel takes us closer to the original words of Jesus than do the canonical gospels. Certainly the possibility that a few of its sayings are authentic words of Jesus cannot be ruled out *a priori*. Their incorporation into the Thomas collection does not *per se* give them any more or less claim to consideration as possible words of Jesus than the other *agrapha* previously considered.

But here again we are faced by the same sort of circularity of argument which we noted earlier in relation to other uncanonical sayings and stories.[36] Nothing in the Gospel of Thomas is likely to be accepted as authentic if it differs substantially from the canonical sayings of Jesus – and therefore, inevitably, any material so accepted is not going to produce any significant change in our knowledge of Jesus from canonical sources. This may seem a rather niggardly attitude, but it is based on the realisation that in view of the Gnostic character of most of Thomas' distinctive material, this document's contribution is likely to be given more weight only if there is reason to believe that the canonical gospels present a distorted picture of a Jesus who was originally more 'Gnostic' than later orthodoxy could allow. So the significance of the Thomas material will depend on our estimate of the reliability of the canonical gospels, and this is a subject we must postpone until the next chapter.

5. The Gospel of Peter

Several early Christian writers mention a Gospel of Peter, though none of them actually quote from it. It is generally mentioned as a heretical document, but it was clearly not too blatantly so, for Serapion, bishop of Antioch about AD 200, was at first prevailed on to authorise its use in church, until he read it more carefully and concluded that it was docetic, and was not by Peter.[37]

In 1886/7 a Greek document, written about the eighth or ninth century AD, was discovered in Upper Egypt.[38] It narrates the events from the end of the trial of Jesus to his appearances after the resurrection, and the author speaks in the first person of the disciples' experiences, finally identifying himself as Simon Peter, the brother of Andrew. It is clearly part of a longer work, as it both begins and ends in the middle of a narrative. When the original was written can only be guessed. It clearly draws on the canonical gospels, though a large part of its material is independent of them. If, as seems to be generally assumed, this was the book Serapion read, it must come from the latter half of the second century at the latest. Certainly the section preserved would suggest a docetic viewpoint such as Serapion discerned, though it is far from the extremes to which Gnostic docetism could go. Altogether a second-century date seems likely.

The story is essentially a free retelling of that found in the canonical gospels, all of them contributing to the composite narrative. Many details are omitted, but there is also considerable expansion, some of it simply in the interests of good story-telling, but some clearly apologetically or theologically motivated. Here, for instance, is part of the account of Jesus on the cross:

> And they brought two criminals, and in between them they crucified the Lord. But he was silent, as if he felt no pain.· . . . It was noon, and darkness descended on the whole of Judaea; people were disturbed with fear that the sun might already have set, since Jesus was still alive, but their law states that the sun must not go down over a man who has been put to death. Then one of them said, 'Give him a drink of gall mixed with vinegar'; so they mixed it and gave it to him. Thus they fulfilled everything, and brought the full measure of their sins upon their own heads. Many people were going round with lamps, because they thought it was night; and some stumbled. Then the Lord cried out and said, 'My power, my power, you have abandoned me.' And when he had said this, he was taken up.

In this passage some distinctive features of this document emerge. Jesus' apparently feeling no pain suggests a docetism similar to that of the popular carol's, 'The little Lord Jesus, no crying he makes'! And the death of Jesus is not stated explicitly, so that the reader might conclude that his being 'taken up' was the 'real' Jesus leaving the earthly body, an impression which might be increased by the altered version of the cry of dereliction – the divine power has left the body on the cross.

Equally obvious is the desire to incriminate 'the Jews', which runs throughout the story. After Pilate washes his hands the initiative passes to Herod, who hands Jesus to 'the people'; from that point on 'they' (the people) carry out the whole crucifixion process – the Roman soldiers have disappeared from the story until they come in as guards at the tomb. So it is the Jewish people who have 'brought the full measure of their sins upon their own heads', while Pilate repeatedly asserts his innocence. All this is historically impossible, but was clearly of apologetic importance to the author.

The above passage also shows an increased emphasis on the miraculous aspect of the events, in the fuller and more 'novelistic' description of the darkness. This trait is more fully seen in the account of the resurrection:

> In the night on which the Lord's day began, while the soldiers were keeping guard in pairs, one pair for each watch, a loud voice was heard in heaven, and they saw the heavens opened, and two men, dazzling bright, who came down from heaven and approached the tomb. The stone which had been placed against the entrance rolled away by itself and stood clear on one side, so that the tomb was opened, and both the young men went in. When those soldiers saw this, they woke the centurion and the elders (for they had come to join the guard as well). While they were describing what they had seen, they saw again three men coming out of the tomb, two of them supporting the third, and a cross following them. The heads of the two men reached up to heaven, but the head of the one they were leading was even higher than the heavens. And they heard a voice from heaven saying, 'You have preached to those who are asleep'. And from the cross came the answer, 'Yes'.

Much of the embellishment is no doubt derived from the story-teller's imagination, but some has other motives. The increased guard, with Jewish as well as Roman members, have become direct witnesses of the resurrection, the gigantic figures serve to heighten the greatness of the risen Lord, and the voice from heaven introduces the second-century doctrine of Christ's preaching to the dead.

The Gospel of Peter is a good example of the sort of development to which the stories of Jesus were increasingly subject; but he would be a bold man who claimed it as historical evidence for what actually happened in Jerusalem.

6. A 'Secret Gospel of Mark'?

We considered earlier two means by which information about Jesus might come to us outside the New Testament, quotations of early records by patristic writers, and the discovery of previously unknown documents. In 1958 these two possibilities were intriguingly combined when Professor Morton

Smith discovered a previously unknown letter of Clement of Alexandria which in its turn contained references to a previously unknown 'Secret Gospel of Mark'.[39] The letter was in Greek, written by hand, probably in the eighteenth century, into the back of a seventeenth-century edition of Ignatius' letters in the library of Mar Saba, a remote and romantic ancient monastery in the Judaean desert. How Clement's letter was preserved from the second or third to the eighteenth century and then lost after the Mar Saba copy was made can only be guessed, but a respectable array of patristic scholars have been prepared to accept it as an authentic letter of Clement. Its contents seemed to Smith so important that he has published a massive scholarly discussion of the letter and its implications[40] as well as a more popular account,[41] and it has formed the basis of his own radical reconstruction of the nature of Jesus' life and teaching in his book *Jesus the Magician*.[42]

The letter is an attack on 'the unspeakable teachings of the Carpocratians', an extreme Gnostic sect of the second century, who were renowned for licentiousness. In particular it aims to refute the conclusions they were drawing from their version of the Gospel of Mark. Clement explains that when Mark first wrote his gospel in Rome he deliberately left out some 'secret' matters, but that later he came to Alexandria, and there added some such materials from his notes, thus producing a 'more spiritual gospel for the use of those who were being perfected', designed to 'lead the hearers into the innermost sanctuary of that truth hidden by seven veils'. This more esoteric edition of his gospel was left by Mark in Alexandria when he died, 'where it even yet is most carefully guarded, being read only to those who are being initiated into the great mysteries'. But Carpocrates had acquired a copy of it, and it was now being used to support his dangerous teaching. In order to arm his correspondent against these teachers, Clement then goes on to quote what the 'secret gospel' actually said (as opposed to the Carpocratians' distorted version of it).

Only two extracts are given before the text of Clement's

letter breaks off. The first is located, according to Clement, between 10:34 and 10:35 of the canonical text:

> And they come into Bethany; and there was there a certain woman whose brother had died. And she came and knelt before Jesus, and says (*sic*) to him, 'Son of David, have mercy on me.' But the disciples rebuked her. And Jesus was angry, and went away with her into the garden where the tomb was. And immediately a loud voice was heard from the tomb. And Jesus came near and rolled away the stone from the door of the tomb; and he went in immediately where the young man was, and stretched out his hand and raised him up, taking hold of his hand. But the young man, looking at him, loved him, and began to entreat him that he might be with him. And they came out of the tomb and came to the young man's house, for he was rich. And after six days Jesus gave him instructions, and in the evening the young man comes (*sic*) to him, wearing a linen cloth over his naked body. And he stayed with him that night, for Jesus was teaching him the mystery of the kingdom of God. And he arose from there and returned to the other side of the Jordan.

At this point Clement adds the comment that the words 'naked with naked' and other things which his correspondent had quoted (and which were presumably being used by the Carpocratians in support of their licentious practices) are not found in the text.

The other quotation is of a single sentence which occurred after the canonical 10:46a: 'And the sister of the young man whom Jesus loved and his mother and Salome were there, and Jesus did not receive them.' And that is all we know from Clement's letter of the non-canonical contents of the 'Gospel of Mark' preserved in Alexandria.[43]

It seems clear from the peculiar contents of the passage quoted that the Carpocratians had found in this document support for some sort of initiation rite, perhaps with sexual overtones, based on an incident which looks like a weaving together of elements of the canonical stories of the raising of Lazarus (John 11) and the young man in the garden (Mark 14:51f), this composite figure being apparently also identified with the 'beloved disciple' of John's gospel (and perhaps also with the rich young man whom Jesus loved according to Mark 10:21, and whose story would thus have occurred shortly before this passage in the 'expanded' text of Mark). Such a conflation and adaptation of elements from canonical stories is found frequently in the apocryphal gospels and the secret initiation tacked on to the composite story is the sort of thing we might expect to appeal to a Gnostic group. None of this need occasion any surprise, if this 'secret gospel' can be identified as a typical Gnostic apocryphal gospel. On that basis there is no reason to give any more historical credence to this material than to any of the other second-century Gnostic developments we have been noticing.

But Clement apparently accepted that the text he quotes (though not the Carpocratians' adaptation of it) did in fact derive from Mark. The relevance of Smith's discovery to our subject thus depends ultimately on how much reliance may be placed on Clement's judgement on this matter. And here a decidedly cautious verdict is in order, for Clement's other writings show him to be both a lover of ideas of secrecy, esoteric teaching, mystical experiences and the like, and also much more open than most patristic writers to accept the authenticity of purportedly apostolic writings such as the Preaching of Peter, the Apocalypse of Peter, the Gospel according to the Hebrews, and the Gospel of the Egyptians.[44] It is striking that Clement's works contain no less than six quotations from the Gospel of Thomas, while no other patristic writer has more than one.[45] Keen as Clement was on opposing what he regarded as heretical, he seems to have been uncritical almost to the point of gullibility in accepting material which chimed in with his own predilections.

So, despite Clement's claims for his Alexandrian version of Mark, it does not seem responsible to regard it as having any greater claim to historical value than the other Gnostic products of the second century. It is hardly an adequate foundation on which to build a total reconstruction of Jesus as a practitioner of magical rites.[46]

C. CONCLUSIONS

We have seen that there is no lack of early Christian material outside the New Testament which purports to give us additional information about the life and teaching of Jesus. Some of it is certainly from the second century, though none can be confidently dated earlier than that. In theory there is no reason why some of this material should not have preserved genuine traditions of the historical Jesus which were not recorded in the New Testament.

But we have seen also that second-century Christian writings are characterised by an amazing range of inventiveness, deriving in part from sheer love of a good story, especially one to enhance the reputation of Jesus as a wonder-worker, and in part from the desire to propagate new ideas and doctrines which are foreign to the New Testament. It is quite clear that second-century Christianity, at least as represented in the writings we have been considering, was not averse to coining stories and sayings 'of Jesus' in order to support new strands of teaching. In particular, the pervasive appeal of Gnosticism can be traced in a high proportion of second-century Christian 'gospel' writing.

In assessing how much historical value may be attributed to this later material, we are therefore thrown back on a fundamental choice between two approaches. One is to take the New Testament evidence (which after all is unquestionably the earliest) as our starting-point, and to use the portrait of Jesus which it offers as our criterion for judging the plausibility of the later accounts; in that case, as we have already noted,[47] the scales are clearly weighted against any significant alteration to our knowledge of Jesus, since any data which do not conform to the New Testament pattern will be automatically suspect. The other approach is to assume that the New Testament evidence is itself tendentious and unreliable, representing a deliberate reinterpretation of Jesus in the direction of what later became 'orthodox' Christianity, and that the 'Gnostic' Jesus of the second-century writings is the historical figure who underlies this early distortion. In that case, the search for 'suppressed evidence' becomes the essential means of progress in our knowledge of the real Jesus, in order to penetrate behind the ruthless and remarkably successful cover-up operation carried out by the victorious 'orthodox' party. This second approach is the one adopted, in various ways, by those who are now advocating a reinterpretation of Jesus as a Zealot, a magician, a practitioner of esoteric cultic initiation, and so on.[48]

In order to assess the value of the writings examined in this chapter, therefore, we need first to come to a decision on the historical worth of the Christian writings which preceded them, those of the first century, as collected in the New Testament. To this subject we turn in the next chapter.

This chapter has discussed only *Christian* accounts (whether 'orthodox' or 'heretical') of Jesus subsequent to the New Testament – and only a small selection of those. It should be noted that purported accounts of Jesus were produced also by non-Christians, designed to undermine Christian teaching. Eusebius (*HE*I ix 3–4) mentions forged 'reports' about the death of Jesus which apparently purported to be Pilate's official returns, and in *HE*IX v 1 he tells how under the persecuting emperor Maximinus (AD 311–313) forged 'memoirs of Pilate and of our Saviour, full of all kinds of blasphemy against Christ', were issued and prescribed for teaching and memorisation in schools. None of these pagan *Acta Pilati* have survived (though Christian ones, no less 'forged', have – see Hennecke vol. I, pp. 444–484). There is, however, an interesting modern example of a deliberately anti-Christian 'gospel' in the so-called Gospel of Barnabas, a substantial Muslim reinterpretation of the life, death and teaching of Jesus, apparently written in the late middle ages and preserved in an Italian manuscript of the sixteenth century. An English translation by L. and L. Ragg was published in 1907, and is now reprinted in Pakistan. As it carries no introduction or notes, the unwary may imagine that this is another early Christian gospel like those we have been considering. There is, in fact, no reason to believe that it has any Christian basis. See further F. P. Cotterell in *Vox Evangelica* 10 (1977) pp. 43–47. A fuller recent study is D. Sox, *The Gospel of Barnabas* (London: Allen & Unwin, 1984).

Chapter
3

The Evidence of the New Testament

Clearly the most direct evidence for Jesus in the New Testament is that of the four gospels. It might be expected, however, that the other New Testament books, written as they were by early followers, in some cases personal companions, of Jesus, might preserve additional memories or traditions, for, as one of the gospel writers himself points out, 'Jesus did many other signs . . . which are not written in this book . . . were every one of them to be written, I suppose that the world itself could not contain the books that would be written' (John 20:30; 21:25). Presumably the same applies to Jesus' preaching – it would be surprising indeed if in the course of (probably) a few years of public and private teaching Jesus said no more than what is recorded in these four slim booklets. Before turning to the gospels, therefore, we must consider the other New Testament books.[1]

A. NEW TESTAMENT EVIDENCE OUTSIDE THE GOSPELS

The book of Revelation is not a likely place to look for historical tradition, in view of its highly symbolic and visionary nature. One may recognise echoes of Jesus' teaching known from the gospels,[2] and note the awareness of the gospels' passion narrative in the presentation of Jesus as the one 'who died and is alive for evermore' (1:18; cf. 2:8), and as the lamb who has been killed but now stands before the throne of God (5:6, etc.). But there is nothing in the book to suggest a historical tradition outside the gospels.

The Acts of the Apostles is in a more conventionally historical form, and contains several examples of early Christian summaries of the life and ministry of Jesus (e.g. 2:22–24; 3:13–15; 10:36–42; 13:23–31). These correspond to the gospel records, but do not add to them. Indeed since Luke had already presented his record of Jesus' life and teaching in his first volume, it is hardly to be expected that he would break new ground concerning Jesus in the second, where he has moved on to the next phase of history. Only in the first nine verses of Acts is the earthly story of Jesus carried further.

Yet we do find in Acts one clear addition to the gospel record, in the form of an otherwise unrecorded saying of Jesus: 'It is blessed to give rather than to receive' (Acts 20:35). This is the most clearly marked *agraphon*[3] in the New Testament, and it illustrates well the possibility we considered earlier that sayings of Jesus might be preserved independently of the gospels. There is no reason to doubt that Jesus said this and that it was remembered and became part of traditional Christian teaching. The same thought, though in different words and not identified as a saying of Jesus, occurs in Didache 1:5; 1 Clement 2:1.

But it is in the letters of the New Testament that we may expect to find more independent traditions of Jesus, as his disciples thought over what they either remembered personally or had heard from those who had been with Jesus.

The difficulty is to know what is an actual allusion to Jesus' life and teaching unless it is clearly stated to be such. Thus, for instance, it is recognised that the Letter of James contains many echoes of Jesus' teaching, particularly of the Sermon on the Mount.[4] But it is only because they are also in the gospels that we can recognise them as such; James does not mark them out as echoes of Jesus' teaching. If then he, or other New Testament writers, presents other echoes of sayings of Jesus which are *not* in the gospels, there is no way we could recognise them as such. In the nature of the case, therefore, it can only be where there is an explicit reference to Jesus' life and teaching that we can hope to find information additional to what is in the gospels. And such references are few and far between.

The letters of Peter offer some ostensible reminiscences of Jesus' life. 1 Peter 2:21–24 reflects on Jesus' silent suffering, as an example for Christians to follow, and 2 Peter 1:16–18 remembers the experience of being 'with him on the holy mountain' and hearing the voice from heaven at the transfiguration. Such references give a valuable new angle on the stories recorded in the gospels, but add nothing to them in terms of factual data.

The letters of John emphasise the privilege of having been a personal witness of Jesus' ministry (1 John 1:1–3), and insist on the physical reality of his life, presumably over against those who were already beginning to think in docetic terms (1 John 4:2–3; 2 John 7). This too, however, adds nothing to what we may learn from the gospels, but merely reinforces the fact of Jesus' earthly life.

But it is to Paul that we owe most of the New Testament letters, and they were written, according to most scholars, before the gospels. They are thus our earliest written witness to what first-century Christians believed about Jesus. Is not this the most likely place to look for early traditions about Jesus? Even though Paul was not himself a companion of Jesus during his ministry, surely a man so captivated by Jesus would have made sure that he was well informed about what his Lord had said and done, and would take delight in writing about it.

The reality is remarkably different. So much so that G. A. Wells' case for the non-existence of Jesus as a historical figure is founded on his study of Paul's letters. He finds them 'so completely silent concerning the events that were later recorded in the gospels as to suggest that these events were not known to Paul, who, however, could not have been ignorant of them if they had really occurred'.[5] According to Wells, Paul saw Jesus not as a historical man, but a heavenly saviour-figure, who long ago came to earth 'wearing a human disguise' and suffering at the hands of 'the rulers of this age'.

This idea, which Wells identifies as in the mystical tradition inspired by the Jewish wisdom literature, was, he believes, only later given flesh in the fictional story of an actual man who lived and died in first-century Palestine.[6]

It is certainly true that not many specific references to the life of Jesus and not many direct quotations of his teaching occur in Paul's letters. This fact has sometimes been connected with Paul's own statement that 'even though we once regarded Christ from a human point of view, we regard him thus no longer' (2 Corinthians 5:16), which is taken to imply that Paul has consciously abjured any interest in Jesus as a historical figure. This is not, however, the natural meaning of those words in context, where Paul is contrasting the old orientation 'according to the flesh' with the 'new creation' which takes place when someone is 'in Christ'. What is abjured is Paul's previous 'fleshly' understanding (or rather misunderstanding) of the significance of Jesus. A continuing interest in his earthly life and teaching is not incompatible with Paul's recognition that before his conversion he had failed to appreciate its importance.[7]

Is it true, however, that Paul is 'completely silent' about the life and teaching of Jesus? Granted that it is not Paul's purpose in any of the letters to give a narrative account of what Jesus did, at several points he does record traditions about what happened. Paul was not of course an eyewitness of Jesus' ministry, so he is necessarily dependent on second-hand information, and he makes the point quite openly: 'I delivered to you as of first importance what I also received . . .' (1 Corinthians 15:3). This introduces a sequence of historical statements about Jesus' death, burial, and resurrection, complete with a list of eyewitnesses of the risen Lord. The witnesses include 'more than five hundred brethren at one time, most of whom are still alive', hardly the remark of a man who was not interested in the facuality of the events – he mentions that they are alive presumably because they are therefore still available for questioning on what actually happened. Paul's own testimony, which was not to the event as such but to a subsequent 'subjective' vision, is carefully

distinguished from these earlier witnesses to what happened
at the time (1 Corinthians 15:8).

Another tradition explicitly quoted (and this time Paul
claims that he received it 'from the Lord')[8] is the account of
Jesus' institution of the Lord's Supper 'on the night when he
was betrayed' (1 Corinthians 11:23–25). His account, which
is earlier than the normally accepted date for the gospel
accounts, agrees with them in its main essentials, though it includes explicitly what is clearly implied in the Passover setting
of the gospel narratives, that Jesus' action and words were designed to be repeated 'in remembrance of me'. The very clear
language of tradition 'received' and 'delivered' in v.23 makes
it hard to resist the conclusion that underlying these accounts
is a pre-Pauline tradition of what happened on Jesus' last
night with his disciples.[9] Of course Paul does not quote it for
merely historical interest, but it is clear that he is grounding
his understanding of the Lord's Supper on the tradition of its
historical origin, a tradition corroborated in its broad outline
by the synoptic gospels.[10]

In other passages there is no specific mention of the source
of Paul's information, but he simply refers to facts about Jesus
as well known. In 1 Thessalonians 2:14–15 (a very early letter,
about AD 50, a mere twenty years or less after the crucifixion)
he refers to 'the Jews, who killed both the Lord Jesus and the
prophets, and drove us out . . .', where the death of Jesus
forms part of a chain of historical events with the death of the
prophets and Paul's own (surely historical!) repudiation
by the Jewish authorities.[11] In Galatians 1:19 he identifies
James of Jerusalem as 'the Lord's brother', thus attributing a
family link with Jesus to the same man (presumably) whom he
names in 1 Corinthians 15:7 as a historical witness of the
resurrection.

In two further passages most commentators are agreed that
Paul is quoting from existing credal statements (or possibly
hymns) about Jesus.[12] In Romans 1:3–4 Jesus is identified as
'descended from David according to the flesh' but also
marked out as Son of God by the fact of his resurrection. In
Philippians 2:6–11, for all the 'unearthly' language of sharing

the glory of God and exaltation above all beings in the universe, the central focus is on the fact that this same person stooped to be a man, a servant, whose obedience culminated in death, specifically death on a cross. If these are quotations of existing formulae, already well known and accepted in the churches when Paul wrote to Rome (AD 57) and Philippi (at latest AD 62), then we have very early evidence for the tradition of Jesus as a real live Jew who was crucified and rose again.

All this does not add up to a biography of Jesus, and it does nothing to refine our understanding of his character or the details of his ministry. But it is surely enough to give the lie to any suggestion that Paul neither knew nor cared about Jesus as a figure of history. He had no personal memory of Jesus on earth, and his letters are written for purposes which give little scope for telling stories about him, but the hints they give are enough to indicate that when he talked with Peter and James in Jerusalem (Galatians 1:18–19) he took the opportunity to inform himself of at least the basic outlines of the historical life, death and resurrection of Jesus of Nazareth.

Again, references to Jesus' teaching, at least explicitly, are not frequent in Paul's letters, but some have been claimed. Among Jeremias' collection of *agrapha*[13] is 1 Thessalonians 4:16–17a, part of a prediction which Paul introduced by 'This we declare to you by the word of the Lord' (v.15). It is not a quotation from any of Jesus' teaching about his parousia known to us from the gospels, so if by this formula Paul means to mark it out as a word of Jesus, it must be one independently preserved. But does the formula mean that Paul believed that Jesus spoke these words while on earth? 'The Lord' is not necessarily Jesus – it could equally refer to God. Even if it does refer to Jesus, is it not possible that Paul is referring to a 'word of the Lord' spoken in the context of Christian prophecy, even a prophecy which Paul himself is now uttering in the name of the Lord (for he apparently claimed to exercise the gift of prophecy, 1 Corinthians 14:18–19)?[14] Despite Jeremias' confident assumption, this case is too uncertain to

class as evidence for an independently preserved saying from
Jesus' ministry.

More significant is the distinction Paul draws in 1 Corinthians 7 between a direction given by 'the Lord' (v.10) and his
own ruling ('I say, not the Lord', v.12; 'I have no command of
the Lord, but I give my opinon . . .' v.25). The 'command' in
v.10 is Jesus' well-known prohibition of divorce, found in all
the synoptic gospels, while the issues raised in vv. 12 and 25
are specific pastoral concerns which did not arise in Jesus'
ministry. So Paul does apparently recognise a difference in
principle between historical sayings of Jesus and his own
advice, however confident he is that he 'has the Spirit of God'
(v.40). Here is not only a quotation from Jesus' teaching, but
also a clear statement that it is to be distinguished from
subsequent Christian wisdom.[15]

The principle that 'The labourer deserves his wages' (Matthew 10:10; Luke 10:7) is quoted explicitly (and as the words
of 'scripture'!) in 1 Timothy 5:18, and the same principle is
given as what 'the Lord commanded' in 1 Corinthians 9:14.
Here Paul again shows not only knowledge of what Jesus had
taught, but also a special respect for it as on a different level of
authority from his own views, simply because Jesus said it.

Here then are some clear indications of Paul's knowledge
of and interest in at least some basic aspects of the historical
life and teaching of Jesus. It must be admitted, of course, that
the harvest of direct references is meagre, though it is also
possible to trace many more echoes of themes of Jesus'
teaching in his letters. But enough has emerged above to
explain the conclusion of G. N. Stanton's careful study, that
'Paul's understanding and proclamation of Jesus Christ did
not by-pass the life and character of the One proclaimed as
crucified and risen.'[16]

But even if the rest of the New Testament does in some
ways reinforce the historical material offered by the gospels,
we have not found that it adds significantly to their data. It is
of course possible, indeed likely, that at many points where
the New Testament writers do not refer explicitly to what
Jesus said or did they are nonetheless echoing parts of his

remembered teaching or reflecting on aspects of his life which are not recorded in the gospels. But without their explicit acknowledgement that this is what they are doing, there is no way that we could recognise such allusions, and so use them to increase our stock of historical data about Jesus. And, for whatever reason, they make few such explicit references – and those almost invariably to events and sayings which we already know from the gospels. In the end, then, it must be to the four gospels that we turn for the essential New Testament evidence about the historical life and teaching of Jesus.

B. THE FOUR GOSPELS

We have now arrived, by a rather roundabout route, at the point where common sense might have suggested that we should have started in the first place. If we have four books all agreed to come from the first century which purport to tell us the facts about Jesus, why have we spent so long searching (with only very limited success) for other sources of information, most of which are of a clearly later date, while those that do belong to the first century do not have as their primary purpose to record what Jesus said and did? Why not begin with what is obviously the earliest relevant evidence?

Here, as so often, common sense provides a much-needed corrective to the rarefied atmosphere of much academic debate about the historical Jesus. If the gospels may be taken at their face value as factual reports of Jesus, then it is clear that they must constitute the essential evidence for our knowledge of him as a figure of history.

But the problem is that for many scholars the gospels cannot be taken at their face value. They are not simple objective records of fact, but highly tendentious accounts, based on traditions which are so suspect as to render the gospels themselves virtually worthless as historical evidence. If you start with that view of the gospels, then the search for other evidence about Jesus, even if it must be later, becomes essential for the purpose of correcting, or where necessary totally replacing, the picture offered by the gospels.

Our task now is therefore to consider the grounds on which this remarkably negative attitude towards the gospels as historical documents has been adopted. It is a long, complicated story; in what follows I shall try to tell it in broad outline, without covering all the details.[17]

1. Scepticism about the historical value of the gospels

From the late eighteenth century onwards there was an increasing tendency to regard much of the contents of the gospels as 'myth' rather than history.[18] An important factor in this movement of thought was the increasing difficulty which was found in accommodating the supernatural element in the gospel stories within the rationalistic world-view which had prevailed since the Enlightenment. An attractive solution was to regard the miracles, angelic appearances, etc. not as facts of history but as imaginary stories which grew up around the figure of Jesus in a context where the work of God was expected to take such a form. Whether such stories were explained away as superstitious misunderstandings of purely secular occurrences, or dismissed as totally without factual foundation, they certainly could not be regarded as 'historical' in the form in which the gospels present them, and so the gospels as a whole came under suspicion.

On such a basis many of the nineteenth-century lives of Jesus were constructed. But at least they still believed that underlying the supernatural colouring the gospels did present an essential framework of the life and teaching of Jesus for those who were prepared to uncover it. In the twentieth century even this belief has been eroded, particularly with the rise of the so-called 'form-critical' approach to the gospels, the most influential exponent of which has been Rudolf Bultmann.

In what follows I shall have occasion to speak of 'form-criticism' as an approach to the gospels which needs to be questioned. In so doing I am referring to the overall approach which is particularly associated with the name of Bultmann, an approach which goes beyond the literary analysis of the 'forms' of tradition to propose a whole theory of the nature of tradition in the first-century church, and of the attitude to history which is supposed to have underlain it. But while this overall theory is one which I wish to question, I do not therefore wish to imply that all the literary insights and methods of form-criticism are to be rejected. Much gospel scholarship on more conservative lines than that of Bultmann has made valuable use of 'form-critical' analysis of the traditions, and I would wish to retain this critical method while questioning the sceptical view of history which has been at the heart of the work of many of the best-known form-critics.

Underlying this approach is the observation that the text of the gospels can be conveniently divided into quite short sections (or 'pericopes') which are in many cases quite self-contained. Sometimes they have clear links with the adjoining pericopes, but each is a clearly defined unit, consisting of a simple story or a section of teaching (which might vary in size from a single verse to a long parable). From this observation the assumption easily followed that each pericope had originally a separate life of its own, as a story or saying passed around in the oral tradition of the church before it was eventually incorporated into the text of a gospel. This view was strengthened by noticing that stories of a particular type (e.g. healing miracles, exorcisms, accounts of Jesus in controversy with the scribes, etc.) tend to have a similar literary structure or form (hence 'form'-criticism), in much the same way that, say, television commercials or children's fairy stories do today; this too was held to point to an original formulation of these pericopes as units of popular oral teaching.

If then, on this view, the various pericopes that make up the gospels were for the most part originally independent, it follows that the overall framework of the gospels is a later invention (usually credited to Mark, as the first gospel-compiler), and therefore it cannot be assumed to represent the actual sequence of events in the historical life of Jesus. Rather it is an arbitrary (though dramatically very effective) plot designed by Mark as a thread onto which he could string his collected beads of oral tradition. In order to recover the historical Jesus, then, we must go behind the gospels, and trace the history of the oral traditions underlying the gospel pericopes, so as to reconstruct for ourselves the most probable original shape of the story of Jesus. In the process we must reckon with the possibility, indeed the likelihood, that the traditions were substantially modified in the course of transmission, as different teachers adapted the stories and sayings they had received to the particular needs of their congregations, and to reflect their own developing understanding of Jesus. No doubt many traditions were lost in the process, and it is assumed that new stories and sayings were added, based not on what Jesus actually said or did, but on what the pious imagination of his second-generation followers thought appropriate to him.

One major exception to this scheme is the passion narrative, for all form-critics have been prepared to accept that here at least there is a generally agreed sequence of events (though with significant variations within it) which the gospels have in common, and which must substantially represent the basic outline of Jesus' arrest, trial, death and resurrection as his followers remembered it. But apart from the passion narrative form-criticism assumes that all that remained to the gospel writers from the days of Jesus' ministry was a wide selection of individual stories and sayings preserved in different Christian circles, often in varying forms, and with varying claims to be accepted as having any basis in what actually happened.

Within this overall understanding of the gospels we may usefully notice a number of specific issues.

(a) Are the gospels biographies?

It has been a settled dictum of the form-critical approach that the gospels are not biographies. In the light of the scenario outlined above it is easy to see what is meant by this statement. Compared with a typical modern biography, the gospels are apparently not the same type of literature. There is no attempt to trace out the main outlines of the subject's education, training, or psychological development. Two of the gospels say nothing about him before the age of thirty, and the other two very little. We are told little about his family, or the circumstances of his life. Instead there is a massive concentration on what is apparently only a few years of activity (though none of them say how long it was), leading up to a remarkable proportion of the book (between twenty-five and forty-five per cent) devoted to apparently only one week, focused on his death. Both in the balance of the work and in the interests displayed, this is hardly biography as we know it.

It should be noted, however, that the 'lives' of great men which were written in the ancient world seldom look much like modern biography. They tend rather to be anthologies of sayings and deeds of their hero, selected with a clear and often explicit intention to recommend him as an example of good living and true wisdom, or to rebut current charges against him. Within their own times then there are rough parallels, at least in terms of literary form, to the gospels as 'biographies'.[19] Where they are distinctive is not in their literary form so much as in their message, presenting not a dead hero but a risen Lord, as the object not merely of imitation but of personal commitment, not a message of recommendation but a radical call to an all-or-nothing discipleship.

But it is certainly inappropriate to approach the gospels as if they were biographies of the modern kind, and to attempt to derive historical information from them in the way one might from Lady Antonia Fraser's life of Mary Queen of Scots. The historical information may be there, but it is selected and packaged in a different way.

(b) How fluid was oral tradition?
Form-critics have tended to draw on examples from a wide variety of cultures and periods to illustrate the way oral tradition grows and changes in the course of transmission. Thus Bultmann, at the beginning of his classic work on the subject,[20] lists as suitable analogies not only the sayings and stories of the Rabbis, but also Hellenistic stories, proverbs, anecdotes and folk-tales; fairy stories and folk-songs

('because the characteristics of primitive story-telling are
even more firmly preserved in their set form'); and 'the history
of the Jataka collection of the Buddhist canon'. But it needs to
be questioned how relevant such analogies are. Folk-tales and
sagas develop over centuries, but the stories of Jesus reached
their written form in the gospels within two generations at
most (see below for the possibility that the time was much
shorter). And may we safely assume that story-telling around
the camp-fire is the right context in which to picture the
tradition being passed on? We shall return to this question
later when we consider alternative models which have been
suggested, which come from a more directly related cultural
setting, and which point in a very different direction from the
free development of tradition which form-critics generally
assume.

It is often pointed out over against the form-critical view
that any significant deviation from the original form of the
tradition would be impossible as long as there were in the
churches people who had been present during Jesus' ministry.
If someone materially altered a story or distorted what Jesus
said, it is claimed, someone would be sure to stand up and
shout, 'No, that wasn't how it was, that was not what he said'.
This is, however, an argument which must be used with some
caution. Much of Jesus' activity and teaching as recorded in
the gospels was not in public, but with a small group of close
followers. Moreover, if you assume that those who told the
stories did not feel it inappropriate to modify them to suit the
different occasions, why should one imagine that the hearers
would be any more concerned to preserve the tradition
unaltered?

But even if the presence of eyewitnesses cannot therefore
be claimed as a total barrier to the development of the
tradition, it is surely true that as long as the apostles and those
who had been with Jesus were around it would be very
difficult for any substantial modification to be widely
accepted, however much the traditions may have been angled
to different needs and audiences, or interpreted in line with a
particular teacher's understanding of Jesus.

(c) Did first-century Christians originate new 'stories/sayings of Jesus'?

The approach outlined above assumes that the first Christians were not particularly concerned about historicity, and were quite willing to feed into the developing tradition stories and sayings which did not in fact derive from Jesus' earthly ministry.

This view is often further developed by pointing to the existence of Christian prophets within the churches. If a prophet spoke a word as 'from the Lord', it would be easy for this to be taken as a saying of the risen Christ himself speaking through his prophet. Such a saying might then be preserv ed as a 'saying of Jesus', and so find its way into the tradition of the teaching of the earthly Jesus. After all, it is asked, 'What is the difference, since it is the same Lord who speaks whether before or after Easter?'

The whole question of the way early Christian prophecy operated is much debated; indeed there is no agreed definition of what 'prophecy' was.[21] So the linking of 'prophets' with the alleged tendency of first-century Christians to create 'sayings of Jesus' is necessarily a rather arbitrary decision. It is put in question by some evidence in the New Testament that a distinction was in fact maintained between what Jesus had said during his ministry and the teaching of his later followers, whether 'prophetic' or not.[22]

Another possible reason for the creation of new 'Jesus traditions' has been suggested in recent discussion, in that parts of the gospels have been classified as midrash. 'Midrash' is a Hebrew term for the interpretation of scripture, but it is observed that in some Jewish writing the scriptural stories were embellished with additional material, often under the influence of other parts of scripture which the interpreter believed to have a bearing on the text under consideration. So it is suggested that, for instance, many or all of the stories of Jesus' birth and infancy in the first two chapters of Matthew and Luke owe their origin not to actual events but to creative meditation on Old Testament passages which Christians saw as fulfilled in Jesus.[23] The whole question of 'midrash' bristles with difficulties. The word itself lacks an agreed definition, but it is certainly not obvious that the fictional embellishment of history is an essential part of its meaning. And quite apart from the word 'midrash', while it is certainly true that over the centuries of Jewish tradition legendary material grew around the Old Testament stories, there is much less evidence for such embellishment of recent history. Furthermore, even if it could be shown that this was a typical Jewish way of writing, this need not indicate that a Christian would have done likewise in telling the stories of Jesus. It is of course clear that the New Testament writers took great delight in tracing the fulfilment of scriptural patterns in the events of Jesus' life, but this in no way suggests that they *invented* those events – indeed to have done so would have made the claim to 'fulfilment' rather meaningless![24]

But whether or not specific reference is made to Christian prophets or to 'midrash', the assumption is firmly entrenched in much New Testament scholarship that the historical origin of alleged sayings and stories of Jesus was not a matter of concern to first-century Christians. On the contrary, a free creativity allowed the Jesus traditions to be expanded with new material which had no basis in the earthly life of Jesus but was welcomed by the churches as enriching their vision of the Lord they believed in and helping them in their discipleship. This understanding of the early Christians makes them sound rather like modern existentialists, for whom, in Bornkamm's famous statement, 'faith cannot and should not be dependent on the change and uncertainty of historical research'.[25] Whether or not this total picture is true to life must be decided after we have considered other views, and in particular the evangelists' own indications of their attitude to the historicity of the material they present, as seen both in their stated aims and in what they have in fact written.

(d) How long was the 'oral period'?
The form-critical approach assumes a long period of oral tradition before any of the Jesus traditions were written down. On the traditional dating of Mark as being not earlier

than AD 65 this was over thirty years, and if the other gospels are dated substantially later, some of the non-Marcan material may have remained in purely oral form for two generations or more.

Two aspects of this reconstruction are open to question. Firstly the date of the writing of the gospels themselves. We shall return to this later, when I shall argue that more attention should be paid to J. A. T. Robinson's view that all the gospels were written in their final form before AD 70, and that the process of written compilation of the gospel materials was going on for a considerable time before the final texts were completed in the sixties. It is interesting to observe that Wells' attempt to disprove the historical existence of Jesus altogether can only be sustained by opting for the latest dates for the gospels which any New Testament scholars will countenance, and by arguing further what hardly any New Testament scholar will accept, that even Mark's gospel was written as late as AD 90.[26] A less extreme 'reinterpretation' of Jesus need not argue for quite such an improbable date for the gospels, but it is interesting to observe that the lateness of the date proposed is often in proportion to the degree of a scholar's scepticism as to their historical value; the cynic might wonder which comes first!

The second question relates to the assumption that until the surviving gospels were compiled the traditions about Jesus existed primarily, if not almost entirely, in unwritten form. Most gospel critics will accept the earlier existence of a written collection of Jesus' sayings (usually called 'Q') on which both Matthew and Luke drew, though many prefer to use 'Q' as a general symbol for tradition shared by Matthew and Luke, some of which may have been written, some oral, rather than to assume that it all derives from a single written compilation. But it is usually assumed that Mark had no written source, and that Matthew and Luke had only Mark and 'Q' to work from. All else was oral.

An immediate objection to this view is that Luke 1:1 speaks explicitly of 'many' who have undertaken to compile a narrative about Jesus, and from the fact that he presents his own

work as in the same category ('to me also', v.3) it seems fair to
assume that he refers to other written accounts of Jesus. In the
light of Luke's statement, one is bound to ask why a predomi-
nantly oral tradition has been envisaged. Is it not likely that
Christians began from a very early date to write down what
they knew of Jesus' life and teaching, as Luke indicates that
they did? The urge to write 'gospels' continued unabated
through the second century as well; need we assume that it
was only a second- or third-generation phenomenon?

(e) Theological motivation and historical credibility
No one who has read the gospels with any sensitivity would
want to argue that they are plain, disinterested records of
facts, written with the clinical objectivity of a modern scientific report or a legal deposition. The gospel writers were men
with a message. They wrote in order to persuade, to convert,
to encourage. They selected their material and angled their
accounts in such a way as to get their message across. The
gospels are, in the best sense of the word, 'propaganda' –
documents designed to change the thinking and life of those
who read them. As John puts it, 'These are written that you
may believe that Jesus is the Christ, the Son of God, and that
believing you may have life in his name' (John 20:31).

It does not take long, moreover, to discover the distinctive
interests and emphases of the four gospel writers, or to
recognise the way in which their books are differently col-
oured in order to communicate most effectively with the
different readerships they had in view. And there is no reason
to doubt that those from whom they received their material
had also in their turn had their own axes to grind.

From this observation it is a short step to the assertion
commonly made by New Testament critics that therefore the
gospels are not to be trusted as historical records – a short
step, but an illegitimate one!

It seems to be assumed that a desire to propagate a message, a theological understanding of Jesus, is incompatible
with a concern for historical accuracy or even for a factual
basis at all. Thus Norman Perrin, one of the most influential

British followers of Bultmann, spoke of the recognition that early Christian preaching was theologically motivated (hardly a surprising discovery!) as 'the *opposite* view' to the belief that it was 'interested in historical reminiscence'.[27] This telltale remark could be paralleled many times in books on gospel criticism.

But this is an extraordinary assumption. By what logic does a concern to preach a message about a historical person exclude a concern to give an accurate account of what he said and did? Can it seriously be suggested that the only and necessary way to draw out the significance of one's hero's life is to misrepresent the facts? Indeed it might be asked how much worthwhile history or biography has ever been written by authors who did not have a deep personal motivation for writing, and a clear and often quite distinctive interpretation to offer of the events and persons they wrote about. Does anyone bother to write a biography of someone in whom they are personally uninterested? Is it not written because the author believes others have something to learn from the subject?

The recognition of the personal interests and even idiosyncratic views of a historian is not in other circles seen as an automatic reason for assuming that the 'facts' he records are not to be trusted. When due allowance has been made for the historian's bias, he is still accepted as a source of historical information unless and until it can be shown that he has either deliberately or inadvertently falsified the record. The mere fact of his personal involvement, even bias, is not in itself a sufficient reason to assume that he has done so.

Why then should the gospels be treated differently? Is a *Christian* commitment and an *evangelistic* aim somehow more destructive of historical concern or integrity than other motives for writing? Many would want to argue the opposite.

Of course the gospels cannot claim immunity from the sort of historical investigation which would be appropriate to other documents which purport to record facts of ancient history. But neither should they be refused a fair hearing on the arbitrary grounds that 'theologians' cannot also be

responsible historians. In following sections we shall see
something of how they emerge from such an investigation.

(f) The search for 'the Jesus of history'
The sort of assumption we have just been considering led at
the end of the last century to the assertion that the 'Christ of
faith', i.e. the object of the beliefs and worship of the first-
century Christians who wrote the New Testament books, is
to be sharply distinguished from the 'Jesus of history', the
man who actually walked the hills of Galilee and died in
Jerusalem.[28] And if that is so, then it must be recognised that
it is the 'Christ of faith' whom we meet in the New Testament
records. The 'Jesus of history' may or may not have corre-
sponded to what the church later came to believe, but in the
nature of the case we can never know this from the New
Testament's own account.

On this basis it is regularly argued that the burden of proof
must therefore rest on anyone who wishes to treat any saying
or event recorded in the gospels as historical. In other words,
we must assume that it is not historical unless it can be
specifically shown to be so.[29]

This assertion has led in turn to extensive discussion of
'criteria of authenticity', that is of tests by which certain
specific sayings or incidents may be shown to be historical
despite the overall suspicion which hangs over the gospel
materials. The most important such criterion has come to be
known as the 'criterion of dissimilarity',[30] which asserts that a
saying attributed to Jesus may be accepted as authentic only if
it is such that no one else could reasonably be expected to
have said it. If it is the sort of thing a mid-first-century
Christian might have said, or even if it would have been
appropriate in the mouth of any other Jewish teacher of the
period, we cannot safely attribute it to Jesus. This criterion
allows us to attribute to Jesus, then, only sayings which are so
'dissimilar' from both popular Jewish wisdom and later
Christian thought that they must express the distinctive mind
of Jesus.

It will be immediately obvious that this criterion necessarily excludes from the 'guaranteed' teaching of Jesus all that is uncontroversial, indeed all that his followers found acceptable! Only the eccentric and the uncomfortable is likely to survive such a test. This bizarre result is compounded when a second criterion, that of 'coherence',[31] is added, which allows that sayings and aspects of Jesus' reported ministry which are recognisably in the same vein as the sayings which pass the test of 'dissimilarity' may also be regarded as historical. In other words, the eccentric and untypical sayings which the first criterion is designed to isolate are then made into the touchstone by which to test all others. The inevitable result is a Jesus who agrees neither with current Jewish piety nor with subsequent Christian faith, a Jesus whose teaching his followers at least failed to grasp or even actively disapproved of.

But surely no one seriously believes that there was in fact such a total cleavage between Jesus and his followers (or indeed between Jesus and his Jewish environment)? In that case what is the point of these 'criteria of authenticity'? In response those who have proposed them claim that their purpose is only to sift out from the mass of gospel materials at least a few sayings which can be firmly ascribed to Jesus. As far as it goes, this is not an unacceptable aim. The problem comes when the same criteria are used, as they regularly have been, to declare that other material which does not pass these tests is *not* historical. The only grounds on which this conclusion could be drawn would be if we had reason to think that the first Christians really did part company radically from their master's teaching. But it is these same criteria which are used to support such a proposal. In other words there is an inevitable circularity about the whole process. If you start with the assumption that the gospel tradition as a whole represents a substantial departure from historical reality, then such criteria may have a place. But why should we make such an assumption in the first place? Certainly not on the basis of criteria which themselves depend entirely on this assumption![32]

Other criteria are sometimes added, based for instance on how widely a theme is attested in the different literary strands

of the gospel tradition, or on how far it reflects the language or
circumstances of Galilean peasant life. Such observations are
important, but underlying these too as criteria of authenticity
is the assumption that the bulk of the material must be
assumed not to represent the historical ministry of Jesus, that
only what can be specifically shown to go back to him may be
accepted as valid evidence for the Jesus of history.

Such is the conclusion to which the historical scepticism of
much recent New Testament scholarship has come. It is made
worse, of course, if like S. G. F. Brandon you believe that the
gospel writers were deliberately offering a new and fictional
view of Jesus in order to obliterate a historical reality with
which they felt uncomfortable. But even without going to that
extreme, many scholars believe that the development from
the historical Jesus to the Christ of the New Testament has
been so radical that we cannot hope to know very much about
the real Jesus from the gospels, and that most of what they do
offer as purported historical accounts is to be treated with
suspicion.

At the root of such scepticism is a general understanding of
the early church, and of its methods of transmitting the
traditions of Jesus, which other scholars have seriously questioned. How likely is it, in the milieu of first-century Palestinian Judaism, that such a lack of concern for historicity, such
a freely creative oral tradition, and such rapid loss of a
historical perspective on Jesus could have occurred? Is this
not to read into the early church the values of quite alien
cultures, not least that of twentieth-century existentialist
philosophy? Is this how we might reasonably expect first-
century Jewish Christians to think and behave?

And so alternative approaches have been suggested, which
attempt to analyse the immediate cultural milieu of the first
Christians and to apply the findings to the study of the
gospels. To some such alternative approaches we now turn.

2. Some alternative approaches

The most radical alternative recently offered to the sceptical
approach we have outlined is what has come to be known as

the 'Scandinavian' approach. Launched by the Swedish professor Harald Riesenfeld in a provocative address in 1957,[33] this approach was developed by his pupil Birger Gerhardsson.[34] In essence it is an appeal to take seriously the fact that Christianity arose in a Jewish milieu, and therefore that any realistic reconstruction of how the traditions about Jesus would have been passed on must be based on Jewish models.

The model which is offered is that of Rabbinic teaching, and the result is to suggest a very different atmosphere from the fluid oral tradition postulated by form-criticism. The teachings, and even the stories, of the Rabbis were treated as 'holy word' (this is Riesenfeld's key phrase), to be passed on verbatim from one generation to another. Gerhardsson has shown in detail how this transmission took place in the Rabbinic schools, which depended on trained 'memorisers' who could recite the traditions verbatim to order. It was essentially an oral tradition, but this does not imply any lack of accuracy. Rather the opposite, for oral tradition was prized as more accurate and authoritative than the written word, and a well-schooled Rabbi could be praised as 'a plastered cistern which loses not a drop'.[35]

On this analogy it is suggested that Jesus, like the Rabbis, deliberately designed his teaching for memorisation, that he expected his disciples to commit it to memory, and that they then preserved it with the same concern for accuracy. The role of the apostles in 'the service of the word' (Acts 6:4) would then be largely as guardians and propagators of this tradition, and the gospels then represent the ultimate reduction to writing of such carefully controlled tradition. In that case, whether the period between the ministry of Jesus and the writing of the gospels was long or short, their reliability as records of what Jesus said and did can be confidently assumed.

Such a totally different approach could hardly expect to be unchallenged. Challenges have been focused in two areas. Firstly, while the majority of Jewish scholars have accepted the substantial correctness of Gerhardsson's account of

Rabbinic tradition, an influential group associated with the American scholar Jacob Neusner argues that the upheaval associated with the Jewish war of AD 66–70 introduced radical changes into Rabbinic Judaism, and that Gerhardsson's material, drawn almost entirely from after that date, is therefore not valid evidence for the earlier first-century pattern. Neusner in fact practises on the Rabbinic traditions a form-criticism as radical, and as sceptical about the historicity of much of the earlier material, as that of the gospel critics we have been considering. In this area Jewish scholarship is at present quite divided.

The second area of criticism of Gerhardsson's approach is in his application of his Jewish material to the gospels. Three questions are prominent. (i) The characterisation of Jesus as a Rabbi, and of his disciples as a Rabbinic school, is questionable. While he undoubtedly did share some characteristics of the Rabbinic teachers, it was the contrast between his teaching and that of the scribes which drew attention, rather than the similarity. As an itinerant preacher, popularly regarded as a prophet, with a group of followers whom the authorities later dubbed 'uneducated, common men' (Acts 4:13), Jesus hardly matched up to the formal pattern of the later Rabbinic 'academies'. (ii) Gerhardsson's account was primarily of the Jewish handling of *halakah*, the legal traditions of the scribes. But most of the content of the gospels is not *halakah*; there are stories of Jesus and his disciples, parables, epigrams, exhortations, and much other such material which, where it has parallels in Jewish literature, would be classed not as *halakah* but as *haggadah* (a very broad term for less formal instructional material); and *haggadah* was not subject to the same strict controls in transmission. (iii) In fact the gospels exhibit a very significant degree of variation in the wording of Jesus' sayings, even of some quite crucial ones. We shall return to this issue in the next section, but at least we may here accept that a theory of exact verbatim memorisation of all Jesus' sayings will be very hard to square with what we actually find in the gospels.

The last two of these objections are in fact appropriate not so much to Gerhardsson's own work but rather to a popular tendency to press it to lengths which Gerhardsson himself would not approve. He does in fact allow for quite substantial variation within the gospel material, and has written at length on the presence of 'haggadic' developments in the gospels, and on the importance of the evangelists' own contribution to the shaping of the materials they record. His thesis was not designed as a guarantee for the verbal immutability of all that the gospels contain, but rather as an appropriate context within which to understand the transmission of at least some of Jesus' teaching, especially where it is more formally and memorably presented.[36]

As for the first objection to Gerhardsson's view of the gospels, that Jesus and his disciples were not a Rabbinic school, a new dimension has been added to the discussion by the work of a young German scholar, Rainer Riesner.[37] Riesner has extended the study from the specialised world of Rabbinic training to the everyday scene of the Jewish elementary education which Jesus and his disciples would have received. He reconstructs this education as carried out in three complementary settings, the home, the synagogue and the elementary school. In all of these, as indeed in most forms of ancient education, he finds a consistent emphasis on the memorisation of texts, with a well-developed system of aids to memory, not least the careful structuring of teaching material into memorable, sometimes poetic, form. He goes on to trace similar characteristics in the teaching of Jesus as recorded in the gospels, and so argues that the focus on memorisation postulated by Gerhardsson on the basis of his Rabbinic studies is no less appropriate to the ordinary Jewish educational scene in which the Christian movement arose. As a 'teacher', who deliberately established a 'school' of disciples to perpetuate his teaching, Jesus thus ensured that his message would not be left to the mercies of an uncontrolled and potentially distorting process of casual oral transmission. 'It is a matter not of a wildly expansionary popular development, but of a deliberately cultivated tradition of teaching . . . So we may examine the synoptic tradition with the well-grounded confidence that it can give us information on the person and mission of Jesus.'[38]

A further movement away from the analogy of formal Rabbinic teaching, but still in the direction of confidence in the essential reliability of the Jesus traditions, is seen in the proposal of Kenneth Bailey[39] that an appropriate cultural milieu against which to understand the gospel materials is that of the story-telling which still goes on today in a Palestinian village. Writing on the basis of a prolonged study and experience of Middle Eastern peasant culture, Bailey argues that the nature of oral tradition is unlikely to have changed significantly since the time of Jesus. In contrast with both the form-critical view (which he labels 'informal, uncontrolled oral tradition') and the Scandinavian view ('formal, controlled oral tradition'), Bailey proposes a model of 'informal, controlled oral tradition'. When the villagers gather in the evening they share stories, parables, proverbs, poems and songs. Some are ancient, classical, widely-known material; others are of local interest, stories of important figures in village history, verses composed by the villagers themselves. The setting is informal, not that of a school or academy. But the traditions are carefully controlled. For one thing, while any member of the village community should be capable of telling the stories correctly, there are generally recognised reciters for each story, usually the more prominent men in the village. Further, only those who have grown up in the village hearing the stories are entitled to recite them. Stories are recited in public, and so are subject to the corrective scrutiny of the whole community. The degree of control on the content varies. Some forms, such as proverbs or poems, are quite fixed, and even to get one word wrong will expose the reciter to public humiliation. In story-telling, a reasonable degree of flexibility is allowed in clothing the essential skeleton with suitable detail, but the overall outline and flow of the story is fixed, usually including a set conclusion or 'punch-line', and any deviation from the accepted form in these areas would be greeted by a chorus of dissent. Thus while the wording and incidental detail may vary with each telling, such variation cannot result in the evolution of a different story however often it is told.

Bailey's study contains many fascinating insights into oral tradition as it exists today in the area where the Christian movement arose. While there are of course important differences between 'church' tradition and stories around the camp-fire, the phenomena of the gospels do in important ways fit this model, in that key sayings and sections of teaching reappear virtually unaltered in different gospels, while there is a significant flexibility in the wording of other teaching and stories, of which the structure and essential points nonetheless remain recognisably the same.

The various proposals considered in this section have in common that they question how appropriate to the real-life setting of early Christianity is the assumption of a fluid and freely creative oral tradition which lies at the heart of the sceptical view of the gospels. All are attempts to suggest what is the nearest parallel we can find to a religious movement which grew up in first-century Palestine, and to offer models of tradition which would fit such a setting. Each of them, no less than the sceptical view, must confront the problem that the Christian community was a distinctive movement, and so its views and methods cannot be assumed to be identical with those of any of the cultural groups we have considered. But at least it may reasonably be claimed that, even if none of these models offers an exact parallel to early Christian tradition, they do indicate that oral tradition in a first-century Jewish context is unlikely to have been the hit-or-miss business which some scholars seem to envisage. Even if very little was written about Jesus for a few decades after the resurrection (and that assumption is open to question, as we have seen), that does not entail that the traditions which found their way into the gospels represent a significant movement away from the historical reality.

3. Differences between the gospels

One of the objections we noticed against a view of the gospels as accurate reports of what Jesus actually said and did is the

obvious fact that where they report the same incident or
teaching they often differ, sometimes quite substantially. Any
theory of gospel origins which fails to take these differences
seriously is clearly a non-starter. But how can accuracy of
transmission be claimed for documents which in fact pose so
many problems of harmonisation?

It is clearly impossible here to discuss such problems indi-
vidually. All we can do is to note some general principles
which bear on the question.

First it should be clearly understood that a serious attempt
to harmonise what purport to be historical accounts of the
same event is not simply a perverse concern of Christian
apologists. Any student of history, especially of ancient history, is familiar with the problem, and any responsible historian confronted by apparently discrepant accounts in his
sources will look first for a reasonable, realistic way of
harmonising them. Of course it is always possible that one or
both is either misinformed or deliberately misleading, or
perhaps simply incompetent. But that is a conclusion to which
a historian will come only after reasonable possibilities for
harmonisation have been tried and have failed. How seriously
the attempt will be made will usually depend in practice on the
historian's prior assessment of the reliability of his sources. If
he already has reason to believe that one of them is not to be
trusted, he will naturally assume that in this particular instance that is where the fault lies. But if both sources are
normally believed to be reliable, he will be reluctant to
conclude that either or both has slipped up in this case until he
has looked at other possible explanations.

Similarly with the gospels. Those who start with a sceptical
estimate are not likely to hesitate long before pronouncing
one or the other wrong or misleading. On the other hand,
those who have a prior understanding of the gospels as
historically reliable records will not be so easily convinced of
any alleged case of contradiction or of falsification of history.
All I want to establish here is that the search for harmonisation in such a case is not an irresponsible putting of one's
head into the sand. It is what any careful historian would do.

The accusation of irresponsibility will stick only when the proposed 'harmonisation' is manifestly contrived and unrealistic, as does indeed happen in some studies of the gospels. But the decision as to what is and is not a 'reasonable' harmonisation is not an easy one. The following are some of the considerations which may be appropriate in the case of gospel stories or sayings.

(a) What is a 'parallel'?

Before suggesting a discrepancy between two or more accounts, it is important to be sure that they are in fact intended to record the same event or saying. And this is often a delicate decision. Gospel critics have frequently taken it for granted that two similar incidents reported in different gospels (or even in the same gospel) must be variant accounts of a single original, and that similar sayings must be variant reports of one original utterance. But is this always the most likely explanation? If Jesus' public ministry lasted for two or three years, as is commonly assumed, it is highly likely that he repeated much of his teaching on different occasions, when the form of it would naturally vary to suit different audiences. Any preacher is apt to use similar forms of expression and similar illustrations in different contexts, and there is no reason to think that Jesus was different in this. Why should it be assumed that Jesus only ever uttered one set of 'beatitudes', which were then drastically recast in transmission into the two radically different sets recorded in Matthew 5:3–10 and Luke 6:20–26? Why should he not have told a story about a lost sheep both to illustrate God's desire to bring in the outsiders (Luke 15:1–7) and on another occasion to reinforce the disciple's duty to care for his brother who is in danger (Matthew 18:10–14)?

And if Jesus' activity was constantly punctuated with miracles of healing, is it necessary to assume that the cure of the nobleman's son in John 4:46–54 is a variant account of the cure of the centurion's servant recorded in Matthew 8:5–13 and Luke 7:1–10? Or when each of the gospels tells of Jesus being anointed by a woman, but with a striking divergence both of detail and of situation (Mark 14:3–9; Matthew 26:6–13; Luke 7:36–50; John 12:1–8), is it beyond the bounds of possibility that more than one such event occurred?

I am well aware that this sort of argument is open to abuse, leading at its most absurd to a doubling of every incident or saying where there is any difference in the telling (including presumably four resurrections of Jesus!), and I hold no brief for such a method. But an approach which is prepared to regard Matthew's story of the wise men as an 'imaginative variant' of Luke's story of the shepherds seems to me as far removed from a responsible handling of the gospels as literature as is the absurdity of suggesting that Jesus twice raised Jairus' daughter from the dead! In other words, it is always legitimate to ask whether two 'parallel' accounts are in fact purporting to record the same event or saying, but it is to be expected that different answers to this question will be appropriate to different cases.

(b) The personal perspective of witnesses

It is a well known feature of eyewitness testimony in a court of law that the same event may be described by two equally conscientious witnesses in such a way as to sound totally irreconcilable. Sometimes they *are* irreconcilable, where one or more witnesses prove to be either mistaken or dishonest. But due allowance for the different perspective of the witnesses often suggests that neither is factually *wrong*. Similarly with sayings, two subsequent reports of the same sermon or conversation may be quite different, as each hearer or participant selects those aspects of it which most impressed him, or which best suit the purpose for which he is recalling it.

But such difference of perspective is not necessarily a contradiction, nor does it render either witness unreliable. Provided that each account is read with due awareness of its author's aims and emphases, which will affect his selection of material as well as his 'angling' of what he records, there is no reason to accuse either of falsifying the record. Again, this argument must not be pushed too far. A difference of perspective must not be invoked to explain away what is a real factual discrepancy. But it is not always easy to be clear which is involved in any specific case, and it is not responsible to issue a charge of inaccuracy or distortion until it has been clearly established that both accounts cannot stand side by side as true reports from the perspective of different witnesses.

(c) Literary convention

The gospels are not the sort of literature we write today, and it helps nobody to try and interpret them as if they were. They must be read as far as possible in terms of the way their first readers might have been expected to understand them.

For instance, in modern literature we make frequent use of inverted commas, and we expect what is included within them to be a verbatim report of what was said. Otherwise we call it a 'paraphrase', and we expect the author to indicate that he is paraphrasing by using the convention of reported rather than direct speech. But are we entitled to assume that this is also the case in first-century Christian writings? Does 'Jesus said', for instance, necessarily indicate a verbatim record such as we would put in inverted commas? At least the question needs to be asked. If the answer is negative, then a verbal variation between the record of the same saying in different gospels is not a real problem for the 'accuracy' of either report.

Or are we entitled to assume that events which follow one another in the gospels are intended to be understood as having occurred in that chronological order? Is chronological order the only permissible way of structuring a 'gospel'? If the gospels are in some sense anthologies of sayings and deeds of Jesus, need we assume that the contents were meant to be grouped strictly in the order of occurrence? Most of the 'chronological' links in the gospels are vague expressions like 'then' or 'in those days'. If then we find events recorded in a different order in different gospels, is this really a matter of error or incompetence, still less of deception? In fact quite a high proportion of the traditionally disputed 'historical discrepancies' between the gospels belong to this category of the

order in which events occurred. How far are such 'discrepancies' the result of our assumption that the gospels were
meant to be purely chronological accounts? Can such an
assumption be justified in terms of the literary conventions of
their day?

(d) The individuality of the gospel writers

Not only are we dependent on the original witnesses and
hearers of Jesus, whose perspectives may differ as we noted
above. We read his story also through four different pairs of
eyes. Each of the evangelists wrote his gospel for a specific
situation, and with his own particular message to convey. The
time is long past when scholars wrote as if the gospel writers
were faceless men who compiled collections of traditions with
scissors and paste. They are Christian theologians, men with a
message, writing to commend Jesus in their own distinctive
ways to their own different readerships. It is hardly surprising, then, that one gospel reads very differently from another,
and that the same story or dialogue may be presented
in markedly different ways. If it were not so, we would not
have needed to have four gospels at all – one would have
sufficed.

But such a difference of perspective is not in itself a
problem for the accuracy of the record each evangelist provides. Again we are faced with the delicate question of where
differing accounts cease to be complementary and become
contradictory. There is no easy rule of thumb here, but my
concern at this point is simply to insist that we should not be
embarrassed by the very clear difference between the gospels
(particularly the quite distinctive style and outlook of John),
as if this were in itself a problem for their factual reliability. It
becomes so only if the difference of presentation is such that
both accounts cannot be true.

(e) Translation into Greek

A further point which applies specifically to the sayings of
Jesus is the fact that most scholars agree that Jesus normally

spoke in Aramaic, whereas the gospel records of his teaching (with the exception of a few transliterated Aramaic words) are in Greek. So what the gospels offer us is at most a translation of what Jesus said – and all translation is to some extent an interpretation, not an exact equivalent. Modern translation theory rightly recognises that the search for a literal, word-for-word equivalence between two languages is not only futile but can in fact lead to serious mis-understanding.[40] What is needed is rather some kind of 'dynamic equivalent', a way of expressing the substance and tone of the original in a form appropriate to the language into which the translation is being made, which may often need to depart quite substantially from the form of the original. In that case, a correct reproduction in Greek of what Jesus said in Aramaic will not be the 'exact words' of Jesus, but an appropriate rephrasing of what he said to convey the same effect in Greek. But such rephrasing may equally legitimately be done in different ways, neither of which is necessarily more or less 'accurate' than the other.

So we cannot expect to find in our Greek gospels the *ipsissima verba* which Jesus spoke in Aramaic. What they may be expected to offer us is rather a reliable record of the substance and tone of his teaching. But it is entirely appropri-ate, indeed necessary, that that record should also carry the stamp of the evangelists' individual interpretation of the meaning of Jesus' words. In the case of John, that individual-ity is most consistently evident, so that there is a distinctively 'Johannine feel' to the teaching of Jesus as John records it. But that fact does not by itself indicate that John has falsified or invented the 'teaching of Jesus' which he presents, merely that in his case the interpretative work which is essential to any good translation has been more thoroughly carried through. Thus John records 'the substance and the deeper meaning of Jesus' teachings as he, the inspired apostle, understood and interpreted them'.[41]

These considerations, then, suggest caution in using the variations between the gospels as an argument against their reliability as records of the words and deeds of Jesus.

4. The origins of the gospels

Our estimate of the value of the gospels as historical records of Jesus is likely to be affected by our understanding of when they were written, and of their sources of information. In other words, how close to the actual events can we trace the material in the gospels? Are we dealing with first- or second-hand reports, or with a folk-tradition developing over several generations?

By far the majority view in twentieth-century scholarship (and for the later part of the nineteenth – it is thus a relatively recent view) is that Mark was the first gospel to be written, around AD 65–70; that Matthew and Luke were both written up to twenty years later, each using as sources the gospel of Mark and an additional collection of sayings of Jesus (known to scholars as 'Q') from which they drew the other material they have in common but which, unlike Mark, was subsequently lost; and that John was written still later, near the end of the first century.

When I was a student twenty years ago this view was rarely challenged. Now almost every part of it is under attack from one quarter or another in New Testament scholarship, though it remains the view confidently presupposed by the majority.

A strong lobby is arguing that Matthew, not Mark, was the first gospel.[42] This view clearly also renders the hypothesis of 'Q' unnecessary, since Luke could have derived the 'Q' material directly from Matthew. But quite apart from the view of Matthew as the first gospel, other scholars who still hold to the priority of Mark have become increasingly cautious of speaking of 'Q' as a single lost document, and many are prepared at most to use 'Q' as a symbol for the non-Marcan material which Matthew and Luke share, without prejudice as to whether it was written or oral, and whether it ever enjoyed any independent life as a collection.

Others are more radically questioning whether a simple scheme of one gospel writer 'copying from' or 'adapting' the text of another really does justice to the complexity of the material, or whether we should not speak of parallel traditions rather than of Matthew 'using Mark' and so on.[43]

There has been, then, a general loosening up of our understanding of the origins of the gospels. And once you begin to question parts of the accepted scenario, it is surprising how much of it turns out to be vulnerable, since the whole structure is essentially interdependent. In particular the dates normally ascribed to the gospels prove to have a relative rather than independent basis, and the questioning process has caused some scholars to wonder whether a significant 'redating' may not be possible, or even necessary.

The most thorough such 'redating', extending to the whole of the New Testament and even to some of the early post-apostolic Christian writings, is that of J. A. T. Robinson.[44] Beginning with the observation that the catastrophic events of AD 70, when Jerusalem was devastated and the temple worship came to an end, are never mentioned in the New Testament as having already happened, Robinson asks whether this remarkable silence may not be accounted for by the hypothesis that the whole of the New Testament was in fact written before that date. Such a radical proposal necessarily involves upsetting the whole relative dating scheme which has become accepted in New Testament scholarship, and thus allows a new look at what sort of writing process is most realistic for the gospels. The result is a clear move away from schemes of direct literary dependence, to the proposal that all the gospels developed simultaneously in different church centres, and that during this process there was the constant possibility of 'cross-fertilisation' between the traditions treasured in the different churches. Thus various stories and sayings of Jesus, some written and some oral, would be passed around as Christians travelled from place to place, and it was possible for four 'gospel' collections to grow up side by side, sharing a good deal of common material but each bearing the clearly individual character of its particular church setting, and especially of the man responsible for its compilation. Robinson suggests that early collections of stories and sayings would be in existence in the thirties and

forties, that by the fifties 'proto-gospels' would have been
formed, and that the gospels as we know them would have
reached their final form by the sixties at the latest.[45]

This is not the place to discuss Robinson's argument as a
whole. It is hardly surprising that a thesis which threatens to
upset most of the cherished traditions of New Testament
criticism has been ignored by most established scholars. But I
must confess to a warm admiration for the man who was
prepared to suggest that the emperor had no clothes, and to a
growing belief that his alternative scenario sounds much more
plausible than the very 'modern' and 'Western' idea of the
evangelists as studiously rewriting already 'published' works
by their predecessors. The complexities of the literary relationships between the gospels have always caused problems
for simple schemes of direct dependence, and perhaps it is
time that we recognised that the process may have been a
good deal less 'tidy'. But more important for our purposes in
this book is the recognition that the traditional scheme of
dates and literary relationships is not sacrosanct, and that
once one part of it is questioned the rest will be affected.
There are few fixed points, and none of these are later than
the early sixties, when the last of the events recorded in the
New Testament took place.

In fact quite apart from Robinson's book there has been a
growing tendency in recent scholarship to propose earlier
dates for one or more of the gospels. A clear starting-point for
this is the strange fact that the Acts of the Apostles finishes
with Paul in prison about AD 62, and says nothing of what
happened at his impending trial. An attractive explanation
for this has always been that the book was written before that
trial took place. But Acts is the sequel to the gospel of Luke.
If then Acts is to be dated in the early sixties, Luke cannot be
later (unless it was subsequently rewritten). The arguments
for an early date for Luke on this basis are strong, but the
implications of accepting such a date are clearly far-reaching,
as it necessarily throws the whole traditional dating scheme
out of gear. It is tempting to suggest that the early date has
failed to find widespread acceptance not because it is uncon-

vincing in itself but because the results of its acceptance would be too uncomfortable![46]

Similarly, while most scholars continue to date Matthew's gospel no earlier than AD 80, so as to allow time for his rewriting of Mark (supposed to have been written AD 65 or later), there are in fact strong arguments for an earlier date once this relative dating scheme can be set aside. In particular, various passages in Matthew refer to details of temple worship, which would be unnecessary anachronisms after AD 70, and one passage (17:24–27) would be positively misleading since it approves the payment of the temple tax, which after AD 70 was diverted to the upkeep of the temple of Jupiter in Rome![47]

We cannot here pursue this complicated question any further, but we have seen enough to conclude that while at the latest the gospels reached their final form within two generations of the events they record, there are strong grounds for suggesting that the gap was in fact considerably shorter. It is, I believe, probable that some, and perhaps all, of the gospels were written in substantially their present form within thirty years of the events, and that much of the material was already collected and written a decade or two before that. If that is the case, we are not dealing with a long folk-tradition, but with four parallel records of quite recent events, well within the lifetime of even a middle-aged witness of Jesus' ministry.

5. Authorship and authority

We have just been thinking of the possibility that the gospels developed as the collection of traditions about Jesus current within different church centres. But while modern scholarship is generally agreed that each gospel reflects the situation and beliefs of the specific Christian community in which and for which it was compiled, it is equally recognised that each was the product of a single author, whose own personality and views, no less than those of his church, will be reflected in the gospel.

One of the gospel writers speaks directly to the reader in

the first person singular (Luke 1:3), and the fourth gospel
carries a sort of postscript in which 'we' (the Christian community?) testify to the veracity of the disciple 'who has written
these things' (John 21:24; cf. also the 'I' in verse 25). Otherwise none of the gospel writers appears directly in his work,
though many eyewitness touches have been detected in their
books, and a few apparently unnecessary personal details
have been claimed as the author's cryptic self-portrait (especially Mark 14:51–52). But formally speaking all the gospels are anonymous writings. Even the 'beloved disciple' to
whom the fourth gospel is attributed in John 21:20–24 is never
named. The headings 'According to Matthew', 'According to
Mark', etc., are not part of the text of the gospels, and are
generally believed to have been added early in the second
century.[48] They thus reflect the beliefs of Christians a few
generations later as to who the authors were.

All these traditional ascriptions are disputed to some extent
in modern scholarship. Luke, the doctor who was a companion of Paul (Colossians 4:14; 2 Timothy 4:11; Philemon
24) is the most widely accepted, as the author of both the third
gospel and its sequel, the Acts of the Apostles. Mark, similarly a colleague of Paul (Acts 12:25; 15:37–41; Colossians
4:10; 2 Timothy 4:11; Philemon 24), but also, if the same
Mark is intended, a companion of Peter (1 Peter 5:13), is
accepted by many as at least a possible author of the second
gospel. But in recent scholarship the apostles Matthew and
John have not had so many defenders of their being the actual
authors of the gospels which bear their names, even though
many would grant them some part in the process of tradition
which led up to the finished work.

Demonstration of the authorship of anonymous works,
whether positively or negatively, is in the nature of the case
unlikely to be possible. There are in fact weighty defenders
today of the traditional authorship of all four gospels, but few
would go so far as to claim that the case is proved.

Is not this uncertainty over the authorship of the gospels a
problem for those who wish to treat them as reliable records?
Is not their authority bound up with their authorship? It is

certainly true that the acceptance of these four gospels as canonical scripture (and therefore as on a quite different level of authority from all the later 'apocryphal' gospels) has often been defended on the basis of their apostolic origin. Even on the traditional view of authorship, of course, only two of the four were actually written by apostles, but Luke was regarded as having apostolic authority by virtue of his association with Paul, and Mark, besides his similar association with Paul, was believed by the unanimous tradition of the early church (a tradition which I for one see no historical reason to dispute) to have compiled his gospel from the preaching and teaching of the apostle Peter in Rome. Does a questioning of the traditional authorship of any of the four gospels then cast doubt on its place in the Christian canon, and therefore on its authority?

Such a suggestion indicates too mechanical a view of the origin of the Christian canon. It is certainly true that in discussions of canonicity in the early Christian centuries apostolic origin was one of the factors they sought to establish. But it was not the only one. Orthodoxy in doctrine was another, and so was the rather indefinable criterion of 'inspiration', which in practice seems to have meant that a book had been widely recognised in all parts of the church as God-given.[49] Thus the acceptance by Ambrose and Augustine that Hebrews was not written by the apostle Paul did not lead them to exclude it from the canon – its place had been won on other grounds.

But in any case it is important to recognise that the discussions of canonicity which we know about in the early church are concentrated in the period after about AD 200, and focus almost entirely on seven New Testament books about which there remained some question after that time (Hebrews, James, 2 Peter, 2 and 3 John, Jude, Revelation), as well as on a few later Christian writings which some groups wished to accept as canonical even though most rejected them (e.g. 1 Clement, the Didache, the Epistle of Barnabas, the Shepherd of Hermas). But long before this time the four gospels were unanimously accepted in mainstream Christianity. Only some fringe groups and individuals had doubts.[50] As early as about AD 160 the Syrian apologist Tatian produced his *Diatessaron*, a harmony of the four gospels, an enterprise which presupposes that those four and no others were already accepted as canonical. Irenaeus, about AD 180, stressed the authority of the 'four-fold gospel', which cannot be either more or fewer, just as there are four regions of the earth and four winds![51]

Thus there can be no doubt that not later than the middle of the second century (and probably considerably earlier) the four gospels were recognised throughout the Christian church as in a class apart from other writings. No other 'gospel' ever came near to being placed in the same category. It is this fact, rather than the precise attribution of authorship, which is the basis of their authority as canonical scripture. Even if it were possible to prove that one or more of them did not derive from the traditional author, this would be no reason to dispute their place in the Christian canon.

For most historians, of course, canonicity is an irrelevant consideration. Their criteria of 'authority' are the same as those for secular history. But here too the credibility of the gospels as historical records rests not on their immediate authorship, but rather on their place as the earliest records of Jesus which have survived, and on the character of the tradition on which they are based and of the communities within which they were compiled. The distinction which orthodoxy has drawn between the four 'canonical' gospels and other 'apocryphal' works is in fact amply justified also on these secular grounds, both of date and of literary character.

Authorship as such, then, is not a major factor in our assessment of the reliability of the gospels. Personally I find all four traditional ascriptions at least plausible, and I believe that the main reason why many modern scholars treat them so sceptically is the prior decision that they were written towards the end of the first century. Once that presupposition is questioned, as we have done in the previous section, the traditional attributions of authorship become immediately more tenable, and I am prepared to argue in favour of all of them, with varying degrees of conviction. But I do not believe that if in the end these attributions are rejected this fact in itself makes any very significant difference to the case for the gospels as history.

6. The four evangelists – aims and methods

While it may be helpful to talk in general terms about how gospels may have been written, it is surely essential also to come to the gospels themselves and examine what they tell us, either directly or indirectly, of what their authors saw as their task, and of how they set about fulfilling it. Clearly we cannot here do more than skim the surface of such a vast subject, but a few remarks may at least help to show the nature of the evidence.[52]

We may conveniently begin with Luke, because he, more clearly than the others, sets out his purpose:

> Inasmuch as many have undertaken to compile a narrative of the things which have been accomplished among us, just as they were delivered to us by those who from the beginning were eyewitnesses and ministers of the word, it seemed good to me also, having followed all things closely for some time past, to write an orderly account to you, most excellent Theophilus, that you may know the truth concerning the things of which you have been informed.
>
> (Luke 1:1–4)

This is a formal, classical opening, addressed perhaps to Luke's literary 'patron', at any rate to an influential person. But this does not necessarily mean that it is a mere formality to gain a hearing, rather than a serious statement of intent. It tells us, among other things, (a) that Luke was not himself an eyewitness of the events he records, but (b) that he, like his predecessors, has made careful use of eyewitness accounts, (c) that he also has access to other 'narratives', written documents like his own, (d) that he feels there is nonetheless room for a further account, in particular (e) one that is 'orderly' (though he does not state what sort of order he has in mind, whether literary, thematic, chronological or what), and (f) that the ultimate aim is 'the truth' (*asphaleia*, that which is firm, reliable, secure). If words mean anything, Luke presents himself here as a careful historian, who has researched his facts, and expects to be trusted in the 'truth' he records.

At the end of the last century the classical scholar and archaeologist, Sir William Ramsay, made a remarkable volte-face. Brought up on the then fashionable view of the Acts of the Apostles as a late and quite unreliable reconstruction of Christian origins, he studied the correspondence of the records in Acts with the complex and fast-changing political scene of Greece and Asia Minor in the first century AD as he knew it from his archaeological studies. To his surprise he found Luke's record meticulously correct, using for instance the correct title for each local official at the precise period recorded, even though these titles changed from time to time so that a later writer could get them right only by the use of contemporary records. On the basis of such detailed studies, Ramsay soon concluded that Luke was in fact a well-informed and scrupulously careful historical writer. In the nature of the case Ramsay's work focused on Acts rather than Luke's gospel, since it was in Acts that Luke wrote of the areas Ramsay knew, but his conclusion vindicates not only the reliability of the apostolic history, but also the claims of Luke the writer to be a responsible historian.[53]

Ramsay's work has been widely influential, but this has not prevented some more recent scholarship from returning to a scepticism about Luke's historical reliability equal to that from which Ramsay dissented. One reason for this is that the bearing of historical evidence is not entirely on one side. On at least one point Luke's attempt to tie in his story with contemporary history raises serious problems, in that he dates Jesus' birth at the time of a census during Quirinius' governorship in Syria, and yet apparently during the reign of Herod the Great (Luke 1:5; the dating of Jesus' birth before Herod's death is made explicit by Matthew 2:1–20). Since Quirinius' known period of office in Syria began in AD 6, and Herod's death is usually dated 4 BC, and since furthermore there is no other record of a Roman census under Herod, whereas there was a famous census in AD 6 when direct Roman rule was imposed for the first time, Luke's chronology here looks shaky.

The immense debate which has taken place over this problem has at least made clear how little we really know for certain about Roman policy and administration in the area during the period of transition from client kingship (Herod) to direct rule. It is at least arguable that Luke's information is not in error, but rather points us to new knowledge in this area (as well as in the only partially documented career of Quirinius). Scholars therefore tend to polarise not simply on the basis of the evidence available but rather according to their prior estimate of Luke as a historian; those who would on other grounds doubt his accuracy are content to regard this as another instance of his unreliability[54] while those who are impressed by the sort of details which changed Ramsay's view tend to give Luke the benefit of the doubt at this point. Many suggested solutions have been offered, not all compatible with one another, and the reader who is not himself well versed in Roman provincial history is well advised to be cautious of espousing one such proposal as *the* vindication of Luke's accuracy. It is more responsible, if less satisfying, to conclude with Howard Marshall that 'No solution is free from difficulty, and the problem can hardly be solved without the discovery of fresh evidence.'[55] But one such unresolved problem in what is after all a very peripheral aspect of Luke's account of Jesus is certainly not sufficient to overthrow confidence in his work as a whole.

It is not so much the question of the census, or any other specific problem of that nature, which causes some today to doubt Luke's historical value, but rather the belief that his aim was not to write 'pure history' but rather to present an idealised reconstruction of the origins of Christianity in which factual accuracy is not a major concern. This is part of that whole difference in approach to the gospels which we considered above, and its roots lie deep in the interpreter's philosophical presuppositions.[56] But there is good reason to echo the protest which is implied in the title of Marshall's book, *Luke, Historian* AND *Theologian*, and to question the assumption that a writer who has a case to present must therefore necessarily be untrustworthy in his handling of facts. It seems fairer to do Luke the courtesy of listening to his own account of his aims and methods (Luke 1:1–4), particularly when in the vast majority of cases where his information can be checked in detail it has, as we have noted, been found to be factually correct.

An interesting recent article under the title 'Luke the Historian' concludes as follows: 'It is of course true that Luke has a case to present, that he writes with purpose and selectivity, that he is not a mere antiquarian. But none of this requires us to believe that he is uninterested in history. Indeed he makes his case through the careful reporting of facts. We must measure him by appropriate standards. We cannot dismiss our best authority because he is an advocate for his subject.'[57]

In the case of Luke, then, his claim is to be a careful historian who has researched his subject and can now offer the 'truth', and while the case is not entirely one-sided, there seems good reason to believe that his performance, where it can be checked, generally matches up to his claim. There may be room for debate over details of the information he offers, but there seems little ground for viewing his account of Jesus as substantially at variance with the facts.

Neither Mark nor Matthew offers us a statement of intent comparable to Luke 1:1–4. Mark prefaces his work with the simple heading, 'The beginning of the good news of Jesus Christ, the Son of God', and then launches straight into a brief account of the mission of John the Baptist as the historical and theological context within which Jesus' ministry is set. His account, like Luke's, is a loosely-connected narrative interspersed with sayings of Jesus, in a few cases collected into longer discourses. It is clear from the first verse that Mark, like Luke, has a clear message to deliver; he is introducing Jesus, the Messiah, the Son of God, and he wants his readers to respond by recognising him as such. In other words, in Mark as in Luke we have the same combination of a historical pattern of writing with a clearly theological 'propagandist' aim. While the two works differ significantly in scale and in the balance of the material (in that Mark includes proportionately less teaching material, and devotes more space to an enthusiastic narration of the striking events of Jesus' ministry), it is clear that they are of essentially the same nature.

Matthew's gospel is distinctive primarily in its almost obsessive concern with the theme of Jesus' fulfilment of the Old Testament. His frequent quotations introduced by such formulae as 'All this happened in order to fulfil what was spoken by the Lord through the prophet . . .' are only the tip of the iceberg. His text is full of scriptural models and allusions, some too subtle to be immediately obvious to the non-Jewish reader who lacks the sophisticated knowledge of the Old Testament and of Jewish tradition which Matthew takes for granted. It is this preoccupation which moulds the introduction to Matthew's gospel, for the first two chapters consist of a varied and sophisticated argument for Jesus as the true fulfilment of God's purposes for Israel.[58] Some have concluded from this fact that the 'events' narrated in these chapters in connection with Jesus' birth and childhood are derived not from historical tradition but rather from creative meditation on the Old Testament by Matthew or some earlier Christian thinker, so that they belong more to the realm of myth than to that of history. Here again, however, the same assumption is involved, that there is a necessary incompatibility between a theological message and a concern to record historical fact. In Matthew's case not only is this assumption in itself unwarranted, but there is the further consideration that a claim to 'fulfilment' is surely rather empty if the events in which the scriptural pattern is claimed to be fulfilled are known to be imaginary.[59]

Prominent as the fulfilment theme is in Matthew's gospel, this is a view which he shares also with Mark and Luke. The three 'synoptic' gospels are appropriately so called not only because they overlap in a great deal of their subject matter, but also because, when due allowance has been made for their

individual emphases and methods of composition, all three
are of essentially the same nature, both in their method of
interweaving narrative with teaching, and in their evident
concern to commend Jesus and all that he stands for by means
of a factually-based account of his life and teaching. What
Luke said of his purpose would be equally truly said in broad
terms of both Mark and Matthew, and what we have seen of
the performance of Luke where he could be checked by
external data (in the writing of Acts) might therefore be
expected to apply equally to his fellow-synoptists, even
though the nature of their historical subject-matter is such
that the same detailed verification is not possible in their case.

With the Gospel of John we are clearly concerned with a
book of a rather different character. But the clear distinctiveness of the fourth gospel from the other three should not blind
us to the fact that it too shares their basic approach, of a
commendation of Jesus by means of a historically-structured
narrative in which the narration of events is interspersed with
substantial portions of teaching ascribed to Jesus.

John, like Luke, has given us an explicit statement of his
aim:

> Now Jesus did many other signs in the presence of the disciples,
> which are not written in this book; but these are written that you
> may believe that Jesus is the Christ, the Son of God, and that
> believing you may have life in his name.
>
> (John 20:30–31)

This statement, while not as full as Luke's, gives us some
significant pointers to how John understood his task. (a) He is
recording things which 'Jesus did', i.e. historical occurrences,
though his account is necessarily selective; (b) he expects the
reading of these narratives to lead to faith, which in turn will
bring 'life' (a word used frequently in John's gospel to refer to
what other New Testament writers call 'salvation'); (c) this
faith is to have a theological content, an acceptance of Jesus as
the Messiah, the Son of God (the same terms as in Mark 1:1).

None of these points is distinctive to this gospel. All four evangelists, to judge by their writings, could happily have echoed every word of John 20:30–31. These words mark John as one who, like the three synoptists, wishes to present himself as *both* historian *and* theologian/evangelist, or rather as one who has a theological/evangelistic message to communicate via the medium of a record of the facts of Jesus' life and teaching.

Thirty years ago John's claim was generally viewed with considerable scepticism. His was regarded as the 'mystical' gospel, an idealised story in which a scarcely-human Jesus appears in unreal situations and offers a gospel of salvation by 'believing and knowing', to which historical events are irrelevant. But the consensus has changed, particularly since the publication of C. H. Dodd's massive study of *Historical Tradition in the Fourth Gospel.*[60] The result has been what has come to be known as the 'New Look' at John's gospel.[61] Instead of regarding John as a very free adaptation of some of the material recorded in the synoptic gospels, the tendency in more recent years has been to accept that whether or not John actually knew the synoptic gospels his work is not dependent on them, but that he had independent information of his own. This means that what had previously been thought to be John's imaginative embellishments of the synoptic traditions are now taken more seriously as at least possibly factual information. As Smalley sums up the new situation, 'It is no longer possible to say that the Synoptics are "history", and John is "theology", so that when John disagrees with the other Gospels he must always be wrong. All four Gospels are theological as well as historical, historical as well as theological . . . Thus John's record of the Jesus tradition, for all its theological shaping, may well be in general terms as accurate as the synoptic record, and at times even more reliable.'[62]

Two examples of different types may illustrate this new confidence in John's gospel as history. In John 5:2ff we have an account of a place in Jerusalem called Bethesda[63] where invalids gathered hoping to be healed in the pool. Until late in the last century no other evidence for such a place was known, and it was widely assumed to be a symbolic location invented by John for the purpose of his presentation of Jesus as the healer. But excavations during this century have revealed in the area indicated by John the existence of two large pools, and of 'a number of small grottoes with steps leading down to them, together with some rectangular stone basins presumably for washing', as well as evidence that in slightly later times the Roman inhabitants regarded the area as a place of healing.[64] As with Ramsay's studies of Luke, the evidence of archaeology has apparently here vindicated John's reliability as a well-informed record.

The other example is John's account of Jesus' trial before Pilate. This is considerably longer and more circumstantial than that in any of the synoptic gospels, and might therefore be suspected of being an imaginary embellishment of a simple original tradition. But a comparison of the details of the story with what is known of Roman judicial procedure in the provinces in general, and of the peculiar circumstances of Judaea in particular, suggests that it is more probable that the additional detail derives from a well-informed circumstantial account of a capital hearing before the prefect of Judaea. Thus John's explicit statement (18:31) of what the other gospels merely assume, that the Jewish authorities had no power to impose the death penalty (except in the special case of a Gentile violation of the temple) accords with regular Roman provincial policy. Other details of the hearing, while expressed in John's theological language, reflect regular judicial practice, while the none-too-subtle threats of the priests ('You are not Caesar's friend', 19:12) accurately reflect the tension which is known from other Jewish sources to have existed between Pilate and his subjects. The involvement of Roman troops in the arrest of Jesus ('the cohort and its chiliarch', John 18:12) is another distinctive detail which rings true to the uneasy cooperation of Jews and Romans in the maintenance of law and order. Altogether to read John's account of the trial against the background of a knowledge of the history and politics of the period is to recognise a well-informed tradition underlying John's clearly theological presentation of the story.[65]

To speak of such a factual basis for John's record is not in any way to belittle the recognition of John's very distinctive presentation of Jesus' teaching[66] and his very clear drawing out of theological and symbolic significance in the facts he records. It is simply to insist that neither in John's declared aims nor in his actual performance is there ground for drawing a distinction in principle between his aims and method and those of the synoptists.

In none of the four gospels does a thorough-going recognition of their theological and even 'propagandist' nature justify us in disputing their claim to be telling us what, as a matter of historical fact, Jesus said and did. There are historical problems in specific instances, such as Luke's account of the census, but these are not sufficient to justify a negative verdict on their historical credibility in general. Again and again, where it is possible to check their accounts against 'hard' external data, they are found to ring true. Where no such external check is available (and that is, in the nature of the case, in the majority of what they tell us) it therefore seems responsible to treat their record as factual rather than imaginary.

7. Corruption of the text?

In an earlier section we considered the differences which occur between accounts of apparently the same event found in two or more of the gospels. Here we are concerned with a different type of variations, those between two manuscripts or versions of the same gospel.

As with all ancient literature, our knowledge of the text depends not on a printed 'publication' of which all copies will be the same, but on handwritten manuscripts, every one of which is potentially liable either to mistakes or to deliberate alterations of the text by its scribe. As one copy is made from another over many centuries, the possibilities of textual variation are compounded. Literally thousands of handwritten copies of the gospels in Greek have survived, some from as early as the fourth century, and fragments of manuscripts, some quite substantial, from even earlier, the earliest being confidently dated no later than AD 125. The majority, however, are later copies, from the tenth century onwards. In these later manuscripts the text is more standardised, whereas the earlier ones show more individual variation. Then in addition to Greek manuscripts there are many early manuscripts of translations made from the Greek into Latin, Syriac and Coptic, and numerous quotations from the gospels in the surviving works (mainly Greek and Latin) of early Christian writers from the early second century onwards.

All of this evidence gives us a mass of information on what text of the gospels was being read by different churches in different parts of the Roman empire during the centuries immediately after the writing of the New Testament books. But in view of the variations between these texts it might be thought that this abundance of information is a handicap rather than a help, for how among all these variations can we ever hope to recover what Matthew, Mark, Luke and John actually wrote?

But in fact the truth is rather that in this area there is safety in numbers. Contrast, for instance, the case of Tacitus, one of the greatest of Roman historians, who wrote a little after the New Testament period. His *Annals* consisted of sixteen or eighteen books, but only rather less than twelve of these survive at all; and of his *Histories*, covering the succeeding period, only just over four books survive out of perhaps as many as fourteen. And for all these surviving works we are dependent on just two manuscripts, one of the ninth century and one of the eleventh. Since these manuscripts cover different parts of the work, at no point in the surviving text (about half of the original work) do we have any check on the accuracy of the one surviving witness to the text. And yet historians generally have no qualms about treating the resultant text as substantially what Tacitus originally wrote.

Our confidence in the text of the gospels should therefore be far greater, for when many clearly independent manuscript traditions all testify, despite differences in detail, to the same basic text, we have every reason to believe that this cannot be far from what was originally written.

It would be otherwise if our manuscript witnesses showed major differences in the texts read in different churches. Differences there certainly are, very many of them. But in the vast majority of cases they concern variations in spelling, minor grammatical differences, an alternative preposition or pronoun, matters which make no significant difference to the story being told or the teaching recorded.

In fact among all the textual variations in the gospels there are only two which throw doubt on more than a verse or two of the traditional text.

The problem of the ending of Mark is well known, in that most of the oldest and most trusted manuscripts conclude the gospel at 16:8, while most later manuscripts add either the traditional verses 9–20 (sometimes with an indication that their authenticity is suspect) or an alternative shorter ending, or even both together.[67] While some scholars still defend vv. 9–20 as the original ending,[68] the vast majority have concluded that these verses were a later addition to fill what was felt to be a lack in Mark's story. Whether that lack was due to Mark's failure to finish his work, or to the accidental loss of the last section, or whether Mark really did intend to finish at v.8, will continue to be debated.

The other longer variation is the story of the woman taken in adultery (John 7:53–8:11), which is similarly missing from most of the older and more trusted manuscripts of John, and which is similarly marked as dubious in some of the later manuscripts which do include it, while a few include it at other points in John's gospel or even in a few cases in Luke's.[69] Here too most modern scholars are at least doubtful whether this passage was originally part of John's gospel, though it is interesting that many are prepared nonetheless to defend it as a historical reminiscence, much like the 'uncanonical stories' we considered in an earlier chapter.[70]

Those two textual questions stand out precisely because these are the only passages of any length in the gospels (and indeed in the whole New Testament) where such doubts arise.

No other major section gives rise to any serious suspicion that it was not part of what the evangelist wrote. Sometimes a single verse, or at most two, within the course of a longer narrative or discourse is similarly doubtful (e.g. the second cup in Luke's account of the Last Supper, Luke 22:19b–20, or the account of the strengthening angel and of Jesus' sweat 'like great drops of blood' in Gethsemane, Luke 22:43–44). A few favourite texts from the older versions of the Bible may be found to have disappeared from the modern ones on textual grounds (e.g. 'Father forgive them; for they know not what they do' in Luke 23:34; or the mention of fasting in Mark 9:29 as part of the means by which certain demons are to be exorcised), and even such a hallowed phrase as 'good will toward men' (Luke 2:14b) in the Christmas story may be lost. Sometimes something previously omitted from the text may be restored, as in the description of Jesus as the 'only-begotten *God*' in John 1:18, or the inclusion of Barabbas' first name as 'Jesus'.[71] But these are minor details which, whatever their sentimental value, make little difference to the overall story or teaching within which they occur.

It should be noted too that while on the issues I have mentioned above there is room for debate about which is the original text, and scholars remain divided, in the majority of cases of textual variation there is virtually complete agreement among textual scholars. Textual criticism is a complex and sophisticated science, which has developed well-recognised principles for deciding between variants, principles which apply to all ancient texts, whether biblical or not. In very many cases a 'variant' is so clearly a scribal mistake (and there are many recognised categories of such mistakes in the copying of manuscripts) or so obviously a deliberate alteration to avoid something which the scribe found either stylistically or theologically unacceptable, that it is scarcely worth mentioning, and no one could seriously doubt which was the original text.

Thus while certain textual problems will continue to puzzle and divide us over details of the gospel accounts, the layman who has no expertise in the rather esoteric discipline of textual criticism is well justified in assuming that the text which the experts have produced, based as it is on the scientific study of such a rich quantity of evidence (which surely must be the envy of textual critics who work with non-biblical literature!), is in all essentials what Matthew, Mark, Luke and John wrote. The student of the history of Jesus is, from the point of view of textual criticism, on vastly safer ground than the student of the life of Julius Caesar or indeed of any other figure of ancient history.[72]

8. Concluding assessment

If we come to the gospels expecting to be able to reconstruct from them a detailed year-by-year account of Jesus' life and work, we will be disappointed. They are not that sort of book. They aim rather to paint a portrait of the man and his significance, by means of an anthology of stories and sayings. They have an overall 'biographical' framework in that, in the case of Matthew and Luke, they start with his birth, and all four conclude with his death and resurrection. There is a basic pattern of development in the intervening chapters of all four gospels, with the initial gathering of a committed group of followers, public preaching and healing, the growth of opposition from the religious leadership, and the resultant conflict which reaches its dramatic climax at the Passover festival in Jerusalem. Within this structure we may discern certain regular traits of Jesus' activity, his well-grounded reputation as a healer and miracle-worker, his challenges to the social and religious conventions of his day, making him in the eyes of the religious establishment a dangerous radical, a 'friend of tax-collectors and sinners', a threat both to the religious and legal authority of the Pharisees and to the precarious political balance maintained by the Sadducees. We may hear his wide-ranging teaching on the kingdom of God, with its new perspectives and possibilities, calling those who followed him to a new relationship with God as their Father in heaven. We may discern his sense of mission, in that in his coming a crucial day of decision had come to Israel, the climax to all the hopes and fears of the Old Testament; and in his willing acceptance of the role of the rejected and suffering servant of God we can glimpse that profound understanding of sacrifice and atonement which was to form the basis of the Christian doctrine of salvation.

All this, and much more, comes to us from the gospels as a compelling portrait of a real man in the real world of first-century Palestine, and yet one who so far transcended his environment that his followers soon learned to see him as more than a man. It is a portrait which we have, in strictly historical terms, no reason to doubt; it is the philosophical and theological implications which cause many to question whether things can really have been as the gospels present them. But we have seen above sufficient reason to be confident that the gospels not only claim to be presenting fact rather than fiction, but also, where they can be checked, carry conviction as the work of responsible and well-informed writers. The basic divide among interpreters of the gospels is not between those who are or are not open to the results of historical investigation so much as between those whose philosophical/theological viewpoint allows them to accept the testimony of the gospels, together with the factuality of the records in which it is enshrined, and those for whom no amount of historical testimony could be allowed to substantiate what is antecedently labelled as a 'mythical' account of events.

For those who are open to the historical possibility of the 'supernatural' dimension of the gospel accounts, they offer not a detailed list in chronological order of all that Jesus said and did, but a rich collection of events and sayings which need not be doubted as accurate memories of what actually happened. The vehicle by which the theological message of the evangelists is carried is not one of make-believe, but of carefully preserved traditions, designed to offer us, as Luke says, 'the truth concerning the things of which you have been informed'.

If this assessment of the gospels as historical evidence for Jesus is anywhere near the mark, then it follows that, however much we may value the material offered to us by other sources, Christian and non-Christian, it is totally overshadowed for the historian by the four primary accounts of Jesus which we call gospels. It must be on these documents that any responsible reconstruction of the 'real' Jesus is based.

Chapter
4

The Evidence of Archaeology

A. THE NATURE OF THE EVIDENCE

All the evidence so far considered has been documentary evidence, i.e. written compositions of the first few Christian centuries which in one way or another may throw light on the life and teaching of Jesus. Most of the more important of these documents have been preserved for us by successive copying of the text. Some, it is true, had to be 'discovered', and in that sense might be described as the fruits of archaeology; for instance, the Oxyrhynchus Papyri or the Nag Hammadi Gnostic texts remained undisturbed in the sand of Egypt for most of the centuries between their original composition and their modern discovery. But even in these cases no one would claim that any of the papyrus or other fragments which have been discovered are those actually penned by the original author. These too are literary works, copied and recopied, but subsequently lost and forgotten rather than continuously used like the New Testament books. It took archaeological research to recover them, but they are nonetheless documentary evidence.

In this chapter I am concerned with 'archaeological' evidence in a narrower sense, with things rather than words. The study of the material remains of everyday objects, coins, tombs, buildings, even whole towns, while it can seldom be so specific in its application to any given figure of history, can provide an important perspective on the story told by the documents, and can help in piecing together a clearer overall picture of the history and conditions of the period in which that story is set. Words are not in fact excluded from archaeological evidence in this narrower sense – there are inscriptions in stone and on coins, which may often have a crucial bearing on the interpretation of the remains with which they are associated, besides the direct information they may offer on the people and events to which they refer. Perhaps the distinction between such inscriptions and the more extensive documentary evidence preserved on papyrus or parchment is a rather arbitrary one, but it will serve our purpose adequately.

Studies of 'the archaeology of the New Testament'[1] customarily cover a wide area, much of which is scarcely archaeology in the true sense, but rather topography or historical geography. The aim of this chapter is more limited. We are concerned only with evidence for Jesus, not for early Christianity in general. There is much collateral evidence for the spread of Christianity in the inscriptions of Asia Minor, Greece and Rome, and much fascinating light to be thrown on early Christian life and worship by the study of the Christian catacombs in Rome or the design and decoration of the earliest church buildings. But our concern is with Jesus himself as a historical figure.

None of the evidence discussed in this chapter is *direct* evidence for the story of Jesus. No first-century inscription mentions him, and no object or building has survived which has a specific link with him. Even if the general location of his burial is widely agreed, there is no reason (other than tradition) to identify any one of the several surviving tombs in the area as his. All this is just what we would expect – an itinerant preacher from an insignificant northern village is not likely to be mentioned in an inscription, and there was no obvious reason for his followers to remember which was his tomb when their faith was based precisely on the belief that he was no longer in it! The enthusiastic production and veneration of material 'relics' of Jesus in the middle ages does not seem to have had any precedent in the interests of the first-century Christians.

The evidence of archaeology will, then, be indirect. It can help us to fill in the background to Jesus' life, to appreciate the nature of the society he lived in, to visualise the places where some of the events of his life took place. Sometimes details of what he is reported to have said and done take on new significance in the light of the background information supplied by archaeology. We shall consider examples of such evidence in what follows.

Before we do so, it would be well to recognise that even the apparently 'hard' evidence of material objects is often controversial. True, 'the stones do not lie', because in themselves they make no claims. But to be of any use to the historian, they must be interpreted, and archaeology is notorious for the widely different conclusions to which experts can come on the basis of the same physical remains. Buildings may be dated to different periods, and what to one man is a temple may be a tomb to someone else. Sociological conclusions from material remains, e.g. estimates of population based on the size of buildings, will depend on prior assumptions as to living conditions. Even inscriptions are not foolproof: sometimes the letters are so damaged as to make the text quite uncertain, and even when a text is agreed its interpretation and reference may continue to be disputed.

In our study of archaeological evidence for Jesus, therefore, it is advisable not to set our hopes too high.

B. SOME EXAMPLES OF ARCHAEOLOGICAL EVIDENCE

1. General background to the life of Jesus

(a) Towns and villages

According to the gospels Jesus was brought up in Nazareth, was based for much of his public ministry in Capernaum, and came to Jerusalem for his final appeal to the people and his fatal confrontation with the authorities. Archaeology can help us to envisage the difference between these three places.[2]

Nazareth was so insignificant that its name occurs nowhere in Jewish literature until long after the time of Jesus.[3] It was a small village, largely devoted to agriculture, bypassed by the main roads which ran to the near-by Hellenistic city of

Sepphoris, the capital of Galilee. Nazareth, unlike Sepphoris, seems to have been a thoroughly Jewish village. Its population has been estimated at between 500 and 2,000, and the remains of its buildings show no sign of wealth in the relevant period. Altogether a very unremarkable place (cf. John 1:46!).

Capernaum was a lakeside town with a flourishing fishing industry. Its location near the border of Herod Antipas' territory made it also a frontier post, with constant traffic through it, and a customs office (at which Matthew would be employed). The remains of most houses excavated are not much different from those of Nazareth, though the traditional 'house of St Peter' is larger than most. None of its public buildings of the first century has been identified (the famous synagogue shown to visitors today is almost certainly later). Its population may have been 10,000 or more. Capernaum, then, was very different from Nazareth, a busy centre which made an appropriate choice for the headquarters of Jesus' mission in Galilee. In this light Nazareth's 'jealousy' implicit in Luke 4:23 rings true. But it was still very definitely a provincial town, not a cultural centre.

With Jerusalem we reach the top end of the social scale. It was the Jewish capital, and the most lasting achievement of the reign of Herod the Great had been to make it a city worthy of its status. By far its greatest treasure was the temple, whose reconstruction, begun by Herod in 18 BC, was still continuing in Jesus' time, though the main construction was finished. It was justifiably regarded as one of the architectural wonders of the ancient world. We shall have more to say of the temple later. But it was by no means the only building which must have made Jerusalem appear to a man of Nazareth as the city of London does to a Pennine farmer. The streets were wide and well-paved, probably laid out in an ample rectangular grid which gave space for much larger premises than those of Capernaum. The city walls were an impressive circuit, punctuated by gateways and by towers; three large towers built by Herod into the wall beside his palace were massive fortifications some twenty metres square – the base of one of them still exists to a height of twenty metres. A great bridge, fifteen metres wide, reached across the central valley to give access to the temple mount from the upper city, while a staircase some sixty-five metres wide climbed up to the temple area from the south. The houses varied in size, but included some which compare in size with the wealthy villas of Pompeii. Overshadowing them all, however, were Herod's two greatest buildings apart from the temple, the fortress of Antonia adjoining the north side of the temple area (which, according to Josephus, was more like a palace than a barracks), and Herod's own palace on the western side of the city. This last was clearly a massive structure, though none of it now remains except the base of the Phasael tower mentioned above. All this, at the time of Jesus, was quite new building, monumental in size and executed with care, using the huge blocks of carefully-trimmed limestone with their distinctive 'Herodian' borders such as the visitor still admires today in the 'Wailing Wall'. It was, visually, a city to be proud of, as befitted the focus of Jewish worship and the seat of the Sanhedrin. With a population probably nearly 50,000, it was a far cry from the solid provincialism of Capernaum, let alone the rusticity of Nazareth.

The evidence of archaeology here gives us an important perspective on the social dimensions of the mission of Jesus *of Nazareth*, as he moves from Galilee to Jerusalem.

(b) Religious life and thought
In an earlier chapter we considered the significance of the Qumran discoveries as 'background evidence' for the life of Jesus.[4] There is no need to repeat that discussion here, but simply to note that Qumran offers us a good example of the way archaeological discovery may help us to understand the world in which Jesus lived, by adding a further dimension to the view of Jewish religion which could have been gleaned from the documentary evidence which was previously available. While it is, of course, the newly discovered documents of Qumran which give us our clearest impression of this separatist group of Jews, the accompanying excavation of

their 'monastery' has added a real-life dimension to our understanding of what life must have been like in the wilderness of Judaea as they waited for the last battle against the forces of darkness.

(c) The languages of Palestine
We have also referred above to the question of the languages spoken in Galilee.[5] The increasing confidence with which scholars speak of a trilingual situation in first-century Palestine is largely the result of archaeological discovery. The texts from Qumran show that all three languages (Hebrew, Aramaic and Greek) were understood in this isolated group (though with Hebrew by far the most used). The subsequent discovery in the same area of some of the military dispatches of the Bar Kokhba revolt (AD 132–135) has shown that even into the second century a patriotic Jewish military leader might speak any one of the three languages.

For the language of ordinary people one of the most important sources of evidence is the inscriptions on ossuaries. These were small chests which were commonly used around the time of Jesus to contain the bones of someone previously buried (in order to clear space for further bodies in the tombs). Many ossuaries of this period have been recovered, particularly around Jerusalem and from Beth Shearim in Galilee, and in most cases there is an 'inscription' (usually fairly roughly scratched, and often misspelled) with the name of the deceased and perhaps a brief epitaph. These inscriptions illustrate how common were many of the names found in the New Testament (Jesus, Joseph, Simon, Judas, Ananias, etc.); they even include, intriguingly, an 'Alexander, Son of Simon', found in a tomb near Jerusalem probably belonging to a Cyrenian Jewish family, and described (in Hebrew) as QRNYT, which *may* mean 'Cyrenian' – could this be the man mentioned in Mark 15:21?[6] But they also illustrate very clearly the trilingual situation; all three languages occur, sometimes with Greek combined with Hebrew or Aramaic on the same ossuary, but it is interesting that considerably more are in Greek than in the Semitic languages.[7] Here is surprising evidence of a more extensive penetration of Greek into ordinary Jewish life (as opposed to commerce or contacts with foreigners) than documentary sources might have suggested. The proportion of Greek is as high as 80% of the inscriptions from Beth Shearim, while the figure for Jerusalem is considerably lower; this suggests, as we would in any case expect, a fuller degree of Hellenisation in Galilee.

More formal inscriptions, such as the famous plaques forbidding Gentiles to enter the temple sanctuary, naturally tend to be in Greek (the normal language for communication with Roman officials in the East) or even Latin (the 'official' language of the empire), but this need not in itself be any indication of what languages ordinary people understood. (I have seen official notices in English posted up on trees in remote African villages where hardly anyone could understand them, even if they could read!) Of more interest is a first-century AD inscription in Jerusalem recording that a certain Theodotus, a 'priest and head of the synagogue', has built a synagogue and associated buildings; it is in Greek (as is also his name)! But other inscriptions on tombs or buildings in and around Jerusalem from the same period are in Hebrew or in Aramaic.[8]

Much other archaeological evidence of varied nature fills out the linguistic picture.[9] Its complexity is rather daunting, in that it is hard to trace a clear pattern of which language is predominant in any one area or period. The one constant factor seems to be that none of the three languages can ever be ruled out as a medium of daily communication. It is probably true that Greek tended to be spoken more by the educated and urbanised, Hebrew more by the religiously conservative, with Aramaic generally the predominant language of the ordinary Jew. But any such generalisation is an oversimplification of what was in fact a very complex linguistic mixture.

So when Pilatus wrote the proclamation on Jesus' cross in 'Hebrew' (was this Hebrew or Aramaic?), Latin and Greek

(John 19:20), he was far from overestimating the linguistic variety among his subjects.

(d) Two inscriptions

Two interesting inscriptions which may have a tangential bearing on the story of Jesus may be briefly mentioned.

The first is a fragment of a Latin plaque discovered in 1961 in Caesarea, apparently recording the dedication of a building by 'Pontius Pilatus, Prefect of Judaea'.[10] This is the first direct Roman evidence for a man known previously only from Jewish and Christian sources (and from Tacitus' later reference, presumably derived from Christians).[11] It also corrects the previous assumption that the rather general Greek term 'governor' represented the Latin *procurator*, which was the title of the governors of Judaea after AD 44; Pilatus' title was in fact *praefectus*, originally a more military title, while the *procurator* was more a financial official. The title does not change the story, but it is good to be informed of the official nomenclature underlying the gospel account.

The second is a decree (in Greek) issued probably in the reign of Claudius (AD 41–54) and said to have come from Nazareth.[12] It is a strong prohibition, on pain of death, against robbing or otherwise disturbing tombs, including removing bodies from them to another place 'with malicious intent'. For the emperor himself to take steps to suppress the not uncommon practice of tomb-robbing smacks of overkill, and it has been suggested that the decree was set up in Nazareth in order to counter the supposed nefarious activities of the 'Nazarenes'; in other words that it is a response to garbled reports of Christians who were causing trouble, having allegedly removed a body from a tomb. There are too many uncertainties to allow us to treat this inscription as serious support for Matthew's account of the Jewish allegations in response to Jesus' resurrection (Matthew 28:12–15), but its connection with so obscure a place as Nazareth is intriguing. At least it shows that the cover-up story which Matthew attributes to the priests is one which would have sounded plausible – such things did happen.

2. Light on some specific incidents in the gospels

(a) The hole in the roof

The houses excavated at Capernaum were one-storey buildings, with outside staircases giving access to the flat roof. The
roof was not of stone, but of wooden beams or branches
thatched with rush and daubed with mud. This explains
Mark's description of how four men carried a potential
patient onto the roof and, literally, 'uncovered the roof and
dug it out' so as to let the man down in front of Jesus (Mark
2:1–4), and the size of the rooms in such houses (never more
than five metres across, and often much smaller) shows how
quite a modest crowd could make this the only means of
access.

Other aspects of these Capernaum houses help to illuminate gospel stories. They are designed for communal rather
than private living, and their crowded layout must have made
privacy impossible, hence Jesus' need to go out of the town to
be alone (Mark 1:35, etc.) Their floors of rough basalt blocks
left large crevices, and the dark basalt walls and small win-
dows explain the problem the woman in the parable had in
finding her lost coin in such a crevice (Luke 15:8–9).[13]

(b) The pool of Bethesda

We have noticed above the importance of archaeological
discovery in confirming John's mention of the healing pool
(John 5:2f).[14] The 'troubling of the waters' which was the
focus of the hope of healing there is perhaps to be explained
by an intermittent spring of a reddish colour which early
Christian writers mention at this location. Certainly the discovery of several pools and cisterns of various periods in this
area testifies to the fact that water was sometimes available
there.[15] (There is no permanent source of water higher up in
Jerusalem than the Gihon spring down in the Kidron valley.)
Whether or not the unusual colour of the water had anything
to do with its reputation as a place of healing, the elaborate
Herodian buildings around the pool (the columns are reck-
oned to have been over eight metres high) testify to its

importance. A Roman dedicatory offering in the shape of a foot found at this site suggests that in the period after the Jews were expelled from Jerusalem it continued in use as a pagan healing sanctuary, and wall paintings of the Roman period in a vaulted underground gallery may support this.[16] Jesus' act of healing was thus a deliberate alternative (and challenge?) to a recognised healing establishment which, whether under Jewish or pagan auspices, perhaps owed more to folk-religion than to a meaningful faith in God.

(c) Jesus in the temple

Among all Herod's splendid buildings, the temple was incomparably the finest. The buildings were totally destroyed by the Romans in AD 70, and the subsequent building of the Dome of the Rock on the site of the sanctuary proper has prevented any excavation of the central part of the complex. What does remain is the outline, and much of the substructure, of the vast walled area, built high above the adjoining valleys, which enclosed the sanctuary, and which was known as the Court of the Gentiles. When the gospels speak of Jesus entering or teaching in 'the temple', it is this area which is intended, not the sanctuary building itself (which only priests could enter) or its more immediate precincts.[17] The total perimeter of the Court of the Gentiles was not far short of one mile, and the area was perhaps six times as great as that of Trafalgar Square. All along its sides ran large porticoes (that on the south side, the Royal Portico, consisting of four rows of columns, the others of two), which gave suitable areas for people to gather in the shade. Here we may assume that Jesus taught and debated, and here were the tables of the traders that he overturned. The 'cleansing of the temple' should not, then, be envisaged as taking place inside the temple building, but in the large, crowded, noisy courtyard which surrounded it.

The magnificence of the temple, both in its size and in its decoration, was proverbial. Even today, the visitor who looks at the Herodian masonry remaining in the Wailing Wall or in the base of the south-east corner of the temple platform can

gain some idea of the impression which caused Jesus'
provincial disciples to exclaim at the size and quality of the
stones, and the rich decoration of the buildings (Mark
13:1; Luke 21:5). A later Rabbi remembered that 'It used to
be said: He who has not seen the temple of Herod has
never seen a beautiful building' [18]

(d) Crown of thorns

Jesus' crown of thorns was part of a mock enthronement
ceremony, in which the royal regalia were caricatured with
whatever suitable material was available (a soldier's cloak for
a royal robe, a reed for a sceptre). A study of crowns as they
are depicted on coins of the Hellenistic period shows that
many eastern rulers of the period wore a crown from which
'spikes' projected outward like rays of the sun. On this basis it
has been suggested that the crown of thorns may have been of
this type, with the spikes projecting outward rather than
inward, and that it could well have been made in this form
using the base of a date-palm leaf with its long, sharp projec-
tions (date-palms grew in Jerusalem then, and they still do
today). [19] If this is so, the crown was an instrument of mockery
rather than of torture.

(e) Crucifixion

The gospels tell us little of the actual mode of crucifixion,
beyond Jesus' carrying his cross to the place of execution, and
the mention of nails in his hands and (by implication of Luke
24:39) his feet. Ancient accounts of methods of crucifixion are
not uniform. But new light was shed on the question by the
discovery in 1968 in a tomb near Jerusalem of an ossuary
containing the bones of a crucified man probably from the
early or middle first century AD.[20] He was apparently fastened
by a nail through each wrist (not through the palm of the
hand), and a single long nail through both heels, which was
still in the bones when discovered. The posture of the body
indicates that it must have been supported by a small wooden
'seat' nailed to the upright of the cross. Both legs were broken
(cf. John 19:31–33). This individual case need not be typical

in every way, but the skeleton does give a gruesome reality to what crucifixion was like.[21]

(f) The tomb

One aspect of the gospel stories for which ample background evidence is available is the account of Jesus' tomb. In the Jerusalem area many rock-cut tombs have been found, many of them from around the time of Jesus. They do not all conform to a set pattern, but certain features are common to most. They are usually multiple tombs, often quite extensive, with several burial chambers opening out from the entrance chamber. Each chamber is likely to have space for several bodies, either on shelves cut lengthwise along the walls or in individual 'tunnels' running back into the rock. In addition there are usually ossuaries containing the bones of earlier occupants, now collected up to make space for further burials. Such a tomb design explains the repeated mention that Joseph's tomb was a 'new' one (Matthew 27:60; John 19:41), where 'no one had ever yet been laid' (Luke 23:53; John 19:41). Burial in a hitherto unoccupied tomb was a relatively rare privilege. It also means that since there was no other body in any of the shelves or tunnels, there was no possibility of a mistake over which was the right body. Hence also the emphasis on 'the place where they laid him' (Mark 16:6; John 20:12; cf. Luke 23:55); it was not simply a matter of remembering the right tomb, but the right shelf within it. The mention of seeing the burial cloths lying where the body had been (John 20:5-7) and of angels sitting where the head and the feet had been (John 20:12) indicates the use of a shelf or trough in the wall of the chamber rather than a tunnel.

All four gospels also mention the stone sealing the entrance. Two types were used, either a 'stopper' pushed into the entrance, or a round stone rolled in front of it along a trough cut for the purpose; clearly the gospels describe the latter, several examples of which survive from New Testament times. Entrances were low, often so low as to require the visitor to crawl on hands and knees, which explains the 'stooping' referred to in John 20:5,11, and the first disciple's pause before entering the tomb (John 20:5).

Whatever the detailed differences between the gospel accounts of the tomb, they all reflect clearly the regular tomb design as archaeology has revealed it, and a knowledge of this design throws light on several otherwise puzzling details.[22]

3. The location of the passion stories

For most of the events in the gospels only a general location – a town or an area – can be discerned, and it is impossible (despite the claims of Christian devotion and of the tourist industry) to identify the exact place where Jesus did this or that.[23] But the events of the last twenty-four hours of Jesus' life are told in some detail, with reference to specific locations in Jerusalem. It has long been the desire of Christians to identify these locations, though in fact all of them continue to be disputed. Here archaeology has an important role to play.

The gospels do not specify the location of the 'large upper room' where the Last Supper was held, and its identification is therefore entirely speculative. The site of Gethsemane, where Jesus prayed, is clear in the general sense that it was on the lower slopes of the Mount of Olives, across the Kidron valley from the temple area; but the identification of a specific 'rock of the agony' is also entirely speculative.

But with the arrest of Jesus we come to more specifically described locations. No archaeological finds to date have helped to identify either the house of Caiaphas or that of Annas. Two rival sites for Caiaphas' house, and therefore for the scene of Jesus' Jewish trial, are offered in Jerusalem, one of which exhibits an underground prison where Jesus is said to have been held, but no such prison is mentioned in the gospels, and neither house has anything to identify it as that of Caiaphas.[24] But for the two main locations of the rest of the story there is more to be said.

(a) The Praetorium

John tells us that Jesus appeared before Pilatus at 'the praetorium' (John 18:28,33; 19:9), and Mark uses the same word of the place where the soldiers subsequently took Jesus (Mark 15:16). John further specifies that Pilatus pronounced judgement at 'a place called the Pavement (*Lithostrōton*), and in Hebrew, Gabbatha' (John 19:13). *Praetorium* is the standard term for the headquarters of a Roman governor. Pilatus' seat of government was in fact in Caesarea, not in Jerusalem, so the question is, which building is likely to have done duty for a 'praetorium' when he was in Jerusalem? There are two obvious candidates.

The traditional answer is that it was the Antonia fortress, where Roman troops were quartered alongside the temple area. This was undoubtedly a fine Herodian building, of which no governor need be ashamed. Excavations there have revealed a large courtyard, perhaps fifty metres square, paved with large striated stones; the courtyard may well date from the time of Herod, and it is natural to speculate that this might be the 'Pavement' – indeed it is regularly shown to visitors to the convent of the Sisters of Zion as the 'Lithostroton'.[25] A further refinement has been the discovery of what appear to be crude gaming boards cut into some of the paving stones, one of which has been speculatively identified as the 'game of the king' which soldiers played during the Roman Saturnalia; this then leads to the suggestion that it was this game of which Jesus was the butt when the soldiers dressed him up in mock homage. It may be so, but this is speculation, not evidence. It is possible, though not certain, that these were the stones of the courtyard of Antonia in Jesus' time, so that if Antonia was the 'praetorium' of the gospels this might well be what John calls the 'Pavement'. But the identification of Antonia as the praetorium is in fact far from sure.

On the other side of the city stood Herod's palace, a larger and more magnificent building, constructed later in Herod's reign. This would seem the more natural choice for the praetorium, and in fact at Caesarea it was Herod's former palace there which the governors so used. Moreover, Philo mentions that Pilatus was based at Herod's palace in Jerusalem at the time of one feast; indeed, he describes it as 'the residence of the prefects'. One of Pilatus' successors also

lived there in AD 66 according to Josephus. Nothing of
Herod's palace now remains, but it is not at all unlikely
that it too had a fine pavement on which Pilatus could
set up his tribunal in public. Thus it seems more likely
that it was here rather than in Antonia that Jesus was tried,
despite tradition which has fixed the *Via Dolorosa* as running
from almost the opposite direction to the traditional site of
Golgotha![26]

(b) Golgotha and Jesus' tomb
The two were close together, according to John 19:41–42, and
so their location may be considered together. Again there are
two main suggestions, but in this case there can be no doubt
about which is better supported. Indeed it was only in the
nineteenth century that the second option was first proposed.
Until then tradition overwhelmingly located the death and
burial of Jesus in the area now covered by the massive Church
of the Holy Sepulchre. Constantine started to build the first
church there in AD 327, and his choice of a site which by then
was inside the city (and therefore not an obvious guess) must
have been on the basis of an earlier Christian identification of
the site. It is likely that a site so central to Christian devotion
would have been remembered, despite the drastic changes
which took place in Jerusalem in the first and second
centuries.[27]

The gospels speak of 'going out' to the place of crucifixion,
and John tells us that it was 'near the city' (John 19:20).
Hebrews 13:12 confirms that the first Christians remembered
that Jesus 'suffered outside the gate'. The presence of several
tombs of around the time of Jesus within the precincts of the
Church of the Holy Sepulchre shows that the area must at that
time have been outside the city (burial within the city would
be unacceptable), and excavations have indicated that the city
walls at that time ran to the south and east of the site of the
church, so that it would have been just outside the walls.
Archaeology thus supports the suitability of the traditional
site.[28]

But the modern visitor, expecting to find 'a green hill far

away outside a city wall' is disconcerted to find at the supposed site of Golgotha a huge church set in the heart of what is misleadingly described as the 'Old City'. Hence the appeal of the recently proposed rival site which stands outside the walls of the 'Old City' (walls which in fact date from the sixteenth century!), and which is still a partly unoccupied hill, with a garden below it. (The description of Golgotha as 'a green hill' in fact derives from Mrs Alexander, not from the gospels, where it is merely a 'place'.) The site was first popularised by General Gordon in 1885;[29] his reasons were neither historical nor archaeological, but are based on literal deductions from a typological understanding of Leviticus 1:11, together with other more 'fanciful' (his own word) reasons.[30] The presence of a tomb below the hill (the so-called 'Garden Tomb') proves nothing, as the area around Jerusalem is well supplied with such tombs, and the design of the tomb suggests a date some centuries after the time of Jesus.[31]

So while neither the actual tomb of Jesus nor the specific site of the cross can be identified, archaeology strongly supports the tradition which locates them in or around the Church of the Holy Sepulchre.

C. CONCLUSION

Only a minute fraction of the objects and buildings among which Jesus lived has survived, and then the selection is quite haphazard, so that the important is likely to have been lost while the trivial has been discovered. In the circumstances no direct archaeological attestation of the life of Jesus could be expected. The best we may hope for is a general confirmation of the background to that life as the gospels record it, a clearer picture of the real-life dimension of the world he lived in, with here and there a new way of understanding the familiar stories in the light of what archaeology reveals of the society in which they are set. And this is what the examples mentioned in this chapter do in fact provide. Sometimes archaeology leads us to correct misunderstandings of the gospel accounts; sometimes it illuminates what was previously obscure; generally it fills

in and confirms the understanding of Jesus' history which
was already available to anyone who read the gospels with a
sense of historical perspective appropriate to the eastern
Mediterranean world of the first century. But its role as
historical evidence for a figure as obscure in his own times as
Jesus was must necessarily be a subsidiary one, while the
documentary evidence provides the main content of our
knowledge.

I stated above that 'no object . . . has survived which has a
specific link with Jesus'. An exception to this generalisation has
been claimed in the case of the Shroud of Turin. This is not in the
strict sense 'archaeological' evidence, since it is not the result of
modern excavation uncovering an ancient object, but rather the
veneration since at least the fourteenth century of an object
which is claimed to have been continuously known since the time
of Jesus; but this seems an appropriate place at which to mention
it.

In recent years discussion of this 4.5 metre length of linen has
blossomed into a discipline with its own Greek name, 'sindonology'! But experts are apparently still far from agreement. The
history of the shroud as a Christian relic, claiming to be the actual
cloth in which Jesus was buried, can be traced back to four-
teenth-century France with confidence. But how it came into the
hands of the de Charny family at Lirey can only be guessed, and
some believe that it was a deliberate 'forgery' around that
period – indeed this was the conclusion reached by the Bishop of
Troyes at the time.

That bogus 'relics' were produced in large numbers in the
middle ages is certain, but many who have studied the shroud
have argued that to create artificially the 'negative' image of the
body on the linen would have required scientific knowledge and
techniques quite foreign to the medieval world, and that the
whole effect is too subtle for a forgery. The wounds discernible
on this image of the body are said to reflect exactly what we know
of the effects of Roman scourging and crucifixion, together with
what appear to be the marks of a cap of thorns and a spear-thrust
in the ribs; and the fact that the shroud was apparently removed
before the body decomposed suggests at least an unusual situation following the burial.

Most scientific tests so far have not ruled out a first-century date and a Palestinian origin for the cloth, though the crucial Carbon 14 test has still not been permitted, as far as I know. But a microscopic examination carried out in Chicago in 1979 is less encouraging for sindonologists; the scientists who carried out the examination concluded from traces of red oxide pigment found in the image that it was, at least in part, painted onto the cloth some time before 1360, so that 'we have demonstrated the Shroud to be, to a major extent, an artist's representation'. They admit that it is possible that a medieval artist 'touched up' a previous faint image, but conclude that it is more likely that the entire image was a creation by the medieval artist. (See the reports by W. C. McCrone and C. Skirius in *The Microscope* 28 [1980] pp. 105–128.)

The whole question is fascinating, not least for the way a sceptic like G. A. Wells has felt it necessary to take the claims made for the shroud seriously enough to offer a full refutation. For if the shroud *should* be a genuine relic of Jesus, it has important implications not only for the historicity of Jesus' death as recorded by the gospels but also for his resurrection. But it would be dangerous in the present state of sindonology to express more than a guarded openness to the possibility that this relic has a higher claim to authenticity than the thousands of others which were venerated in the fourteenth century.

For a full discussion by a 'convert' to the authenticity of the shroud see I. Wilson, *The Shroud of Turin* (New York: Doubleday, 1978); more briefly E. L. Mascall, *Whatever Happened to the Human Mind?* (London: SPCK, 1980) pp. 60–63. For a careful statement of the case against, see G. A. Wells, *The Historical Evidence for Jesus*, pp. 183–195.

Chapter
5

Jesus in History

A NEW IMAGE?

In the television series referred to above,[1] *Jesus – the Evidence*, there was a repeated sequence in which a plaster image of Jesus was dramatically exploded. It was a very traditional image (appropriately described by one critic as 'kitsch') of a white-faced Jesus with long, wavy hair and a rather sickly expression. As the pieces of this shattered 'Jesus' floated in slow motion across the screen, we were invited to consider the possibility that our old image of Jesus was now destroyed beyond repair by historical investigation, and that it was time to adopt a new one.

It was, perhaps, not in the best of taste, and some were understandably offended. But even if this was not the most diplomatic way to make the point, was there not a point worth making? How much of our traditional understanding of Jesus is the product not so much of the historical records as of pious imagination and sentimentality? How much of it has the effect of turning Jesus into a man of our own culture, or, still worse, of no culture at all, thus effectively cutting him off from real life? How many people today, Christian people included, subconsciously think of Jesus in the terms of the Christianised version of the *Testimonium Flavianum*: 'a wise man, if indeed one should call him a man'? Are we not still slightly shocked at the thought that Jesus could have had a real sense of humour, or held political views?

The preceding chapters have given reason for taking the New Testament accounts seriously as historical evidence both for specific words and deeds of Jesus and for our overall understanding of the sort of person he was. But in the course of Christian history much has been superimposed on that New Testament evidence, beginning with the growth of apocryphal gospels in the second century, and continuing as each age has added its own distinctive veneer to the portrait. At some points the New Testament records have come to be misinterpreted; at many points they have been overlaid by Christian tradition. It is not always easy for Christians today to distinguish between what is presented in the New Testament and what subsequent devotion has added to the picture.

The point was rather painfully illustrated for me when I wrote a brief article for a Christian magazine pointing out that the Bible nowhere says that Jesus was born in a stable, and that the traditional scene in western Christianity of rejection from 'the inn' is based on what is probably a mistranslation of the Greek word *katalyma*, which more usually means a 'guest-room' (of a private house). I suggested that Luke's account is better understood of the birth of Jesus in the homely, happy atmosphere of a normal peasant home, 'the Palestinian equivalent of a two-bedroom semi'. I thus hoped to rescue the story of Jesus' birth from 'the make-believe world of Christmas cards and medieval carols', and to present him, as I believe the New Testament does, as truly 'one of us', in his birth as in his life.[2]

The article was published just before Christmas, and was noticed and commented on in one of the Sunday newspapers. This quickly led to a series of radio interviews, in which I was cast in the role of the theological spoil-sport, who wants to destroy the one bit of the Bible story which everyone knows and loves. My aim had been the constructive one of reinforcing the human reality of Jesus' birth by peeling away an unnecessary (and unbiblical) layer of sentimental tradition. But my interviewers seemed unable to distinguish between what was biblical and what was traditional. For them an 'attack' on any aspect of the traditional Christmas scene was an attack on essential Christian truth.

I suppose the situation was not helped by the fact that my

article coincided with the controversy over the questioning by the Bishop of Durham of the doctrines of the virgin conception and the bodily resurrection of Jesus. But it was disconcerting to find my attempts to restore a true understanding of the New Testament account of Jesus' birth equated with his 'demythologising' of the plain teaching of that same New Testament! The lesson for me was that, to a greater extent than we often realise, we mistake that which is familiar for that which is true.

Now I have no desire to disturb traditional ideas simply for the sake of novelty. But when a developing 'mythology' threatens to obscure the New Testament evidence (and nowhere is this more so than in the Christmas story, with its sentimental appeal reaching far outside professing Christian circles), it seems to me important that we stop and question how much is primary historical evidence and how much is post-biblical accretion. If in the process we discover that some well-loved carols do not fit the biblical scene, that is a small price to pay for the rediscovery of a Jesus who in his birth as in his subsequent life and death enters fully into a real human situation.

Historical evidence of the sort we have been examining in this book may affect our traditional understanding of Jesus in important ways. An increasing awareness of the world in which he lived, and of the sort of people who were to be found in it, can help us at many points to read the New Testament accounts of Jesus with fuller understanding, as he comes more into focus in the context of the real-life situation of first-century Palestine. The result, even if it modifies some of our traditional views, can only be that Jesus becomes less of a plaster figure and more of a real human being. In view of the unconscious tendency of much popular Christianity towards docetism (a view of Jesus which sees his humanity as only skin-deep) this is a result to be welcomed.

JESUS IN HIS TIMES

We have seen, for instance, what it meant in first-century Palestine to be a Galilean, especially when confronting the official Jewish establishment in Jerusalem. And even in Galilee there was a significant social difference between a man of Nazareth and one from Capernaum. We have seen how the ordinary Jew might have identified Jesus during his Galilean ministry, at least on first acquaintance, more with a miracle-working 'holy man' like Hanina ben Dosa than with a more orthodox Rabbi. An itinerant teacher who depended for his daily bread on the hospitality of his supporters and the gifts of well-wishers must have seemed eccentric in a culture which expected its religious teachers to experience the material blessing of God as a mark of their piety.[3] Moreover, a religious teacher who was not reluctant to contract ritual defilement by associating with 'tax-collectors and sinners', and whose teaching questioned many of the fundamental scribal rules for holy living, could not be expected to find a ready welcome among the religious establishment. As for the much stricter régime of the men of Qumran, for whom even the Jerusalem priesthood was hopelessly compromised, we can imagine how they would have reacted against Jesus if he had come to their notice (though there is no reason to believe that he ever did).

In the political ferment of Palestine under Roman rule again Jesus must have been a conspicuous figure. A man who presented himself, however guardedly, as the Messiah of Israel could not avoid comparison with other would-be liberators of the people of God, and there is ample evidence in the New Testament that many of his followers understood his mission in strongly nationalistic and political terms. The crowds who hailed him on his arrival in Jerusalem as the Son of David, and looked for 'the coming kingdom of our father David' (Mark 11:10), were surely not thinking primarily in terms of a theology of spiritual redemption! There was enough plausibility in the charge of insurrection to convince the Roman prefect that Jesus should be executed along with other 'freedom fighters'.

Yet it is equally clear from the New Testament that Jesus not only refused the political role which his followers wanted to confer on him,[4] and went out of his way to distance himself from 'zealot' ideals (e.g. Matthew 5:41; Mark 12:13–17), but he also preached a message not of liberation for the Jews and their capital, but rather of destruction. His repeated threats of judgement to fall on 'this evil generation' were balanced by his prediction that people 'from east and west' would come into the messianic banquet, while Jews (who assumed they would be there by right) would find themselves excluded (Matthew 8:11–12). Several of his parables focus on the rejection of those who regarded themselves as the people of God, and their replacement by those they despised (especially the striking sequence of three parables directed against the official Jewish leadership in Matthew 21:28–22:14).

But perhaps his most offensive message was his sustained attack on the temple. As the focus of national worship, and therefore of the corporate identity of Israel as the people of God, the temple in Jerusalem was a symbol of national pride and aspiration. Yet Jesus declared that it was to be superseded by 'something greater' (Matthew 12:6), himself carried out a dramatic 'demonstration' in its precincts which unmistakably repudiated its existing régime and set himself over it as the Messiah (Mark 11:15–18 and parallels), declared that it was soon to be totally destroyed (Matthew 23:38; 24:2), and at his trial refused to deny the charge that he had threatened to pull it down himself in order to rebuild it (Matthew 26:60–63; cf. 27:40; Acts 6:13–14). A recent study by E. P. Sanders has rightly concluded that, whatever other causes of offence there may have been in Jesus' life and teaching, his attack on the temple must inevitably have alienated him from all main sectors of Jewish society, and was one of the chief causes of his ultimate execution.[5]

Some thirty years after the death of Jesus there was another Jewish 'prophet' whose public image must in some ways have been remarkably similar. He too was called Jesus, and he, like his namesake, came to the notice of the Roman governor as a prophet of doom whose message was unpopular with the Jewish authorities.

Four years before the war, when the city was particularly peaceful and prosperous, a certain Jesus, son of Hananiah, an uneducated countryman, came to the festival at which it is the custom for everyone to make tabernacles for God. In the temple he suddenly began to cry out, 'A voice from the east, a voice from the west, a voice from the four winds, a voice against Jerusalem and the sanctuary, a voice against bridegrooms and brides, a voice against the whole people.' Day and night he went about all the streets shouting like this. Some of the civic leaders were furious at this ominous language, and arrested the man and gave him a severe beating. But, instead of making any plea on his own behalf, or appealing to those who were beating him, he just kept on shouting the same words. So the authorities, rightly supposing that the man was moved by some supernatural power, referred him to the Roman governor. There he was flogged until the bones were laid bare, but still he made no appeal, nor even wept at all, but with the most piteous tone of voice imaginable he reacted to each blow with 'Woe to Jerusalem'. Albinus, who was procurator at the time, questioned him about who he was and where he came from, and why he was making all this fuss, but he gave him no answer at all, and instead went on repeating his lament over the city. In the end Albinus decided he was mad, and released him.

(Josephus, *BJ* VI 300–305)

Josephus goes on to say that this unprepossessing character went on with his one-man 'mission' for seven and a half years until he was killed in the siege of Jerusalem, having seen his threats amply fulfilled.

Pilatus, faced with the earlier Jesus and his unpopular message, would have liked to do as his later successor did, to treat him as a harmless fanatic, a nuisance but not a real danger. 'I will therefore chastise him and release him' (Luke 23:22). But Jesus had made himself even more unpopular with the authorities than his later namesake, and Pilatus, perhaps more vulnerable than Albinus, had to take more drastic action.

To the unsympathetic outsider, then, Jesus of Nazareth may well have appeared much as this later Jesus did. Of course there was much more to his teaching and his activity than simply a repeated message of doom, but this would have been what impressed, and offended, a casual observer in Jerusalem. It was only those who spent time with Jesus, and listened to his teaching, who were able to penetrate beyond the image of the prophet of doom to see the whole new way of life, and the new basis of relationship with God, that he offered. No wonder Jesus' ministry left people deeply divided in their estimate of him and of his teaching.

That teaching was focused on the proclamation of the 'kingship of God'. (The word 'kingdom', traditionally used in English translations of the Greek *basileia*, is misleading as it suggests a place or a group of people, whereas *basileia* is an abstract noun indicating 'rule', 'reign', 'sovereignty'.)[6] All Jews believed that God, as the creator, was by right 'king of the universe', and the prophecies of the Old Testament had taught them to look forward to the day when God's kingship would be firmly and finally established on earth, when his people Israel would again enjoy the pre-eminence which was theirs by right. When Jesus began proclaiming in Galilee, 'The time is fulfilled and the kingship of God has come near' (Mark 1:15), it is not hard to imagine what most people thought, and the periodical emergence in the gospel records of popular messianic enthusiasm no doubt reflects a major current in the response to Jesus, at least in the early days before he fell foul of the authorities and began to preach judgement on Jerusalem.

But among his closer followers it soon became apparent that Jesus' idea of God's kingship was on a different plane altogether from the patriotic feelings his preaching had evoked. It demanded a total rethinking of their inherited theology and their sense of national pride. It made room for tax-collectors and sinners, for women and children, for Gentiles, Samaritans, and other undesirables. It offered a place to the poor and disadvantaged. But it had no place for the smug and self-satisfied, and could even envisage the ultimate rejection of the 'sons of the kingdom', those who saw God's eschatological blessings as theirs by right.

To take seriously Jesus' teaching (and to make sense of his activity, in which that teaching found visible expression)

demanded a radical reorientation, an abandonment of cherished preconceptions, a questioning of conventional values
and attitudes. It called men and women to decision, a decision
which made them potentially the outcasts of Jewish society. It
was a potent, disturbing, divisive message, very different
from the milk-and-water doctrine of the universal brotherhood of man which some modern thought has foisted onto
Jesus. But it was also the source of hope, of restoration, of the
effective kingship of God among his people. It was the
message which launched the world's greatest religion.

A historical reconstruction of Jesus which cannot explain
all this is a non-starter.

HISTORICAL REALISM

But this is not the place to attempt such a reconstruction.
What I hope this book has done is to indicate how a study of
the historical evidence for Jesus and for the times in which he
lived can enable us to picture him more realistically as a
three-dimensional figure in history, a first-century Palestinian
Jew living within the same social, political and religious
currents which we can trace through the writings of Josephus
and of the Rabbis, and which are illustrated in intriguing if
fragmentary detail by the results of archaeological discovery.
If in the process we lose some of the familiar features which
tradition has added to the portrait of Jesus, I do not believe
this should be a cause for regret. We may indeed find that the
old plaster image is shattered. But if that image was not the
Jesus of the New Testament (who is the only Jesus of
Nazareth known to history), I do not believe that it was worth
preserving.

In earlier chapters we have noticed the tendency of some
recent writers to try to go behind the New Testament portrait
of Jesus, in search of a more 'real' Jesus who even by the time
the New Testament documents were written had been largely
forgotten and replaced by a semi-mythical figure, the 'Christ
of faith'. We have seen repeatedly that the evidence on which
such reconstructions are based (when they are not mere

unsupported speculation) is in fact later in date than the New Testament writings, and can generally be identified with what by the second century were regarded as heretical movements, deviations from the original Christian message, usually in the direction of a faith more appealing to the philosophical or religious climate of the day. The only justification for preferring this later material to the earliest sources available to us is the belief that a profound change in the understanding of Jesus had taken place between his lifetime and the time when the New Testament books were written. But in our consideration of the New Testament evidence we have seen ample reason to question this assumption, and to accept the gospels as responsible, historically-grounded presentations of a tradition which leaves no room for the major volte-face among the majority of early Christians which many recent theories suppose.

So in our search for the historical Jesus we need to avoid two equally irresponsible extremes.

One extreme is the naive assumption that all we have traditionally believed about Jesus corresponds to historical reality. It does not take much observation of the Christian scene today to realise that this cannot be the case, for very different and indeed mutually exclusive images of Jesus are cherished with equal sincerity by different Christian groups – not to mention the many other images which earlier generations have venerated. The remedy against this extreme is to foster a conscious distinction between what may be supported from the New Testament, interpreted with due regard to its wider historical context, and what is merely the product of Christian tradition, however sincerely motivated – and a willingness to allow the former to stand in judgement over the latter.

But the other extreme is the over-enthusiastic iconoclasm which distrusts the evidence of the New Testament as well, not because it has access to any records closer to the events, but because it finds the Jesus of the New Testament unacceptable, even if he can be discarded only by appealing to supposedly 'suppressed evidence' which in fact cannot be traced any earlier than the Gnostic movements of the second century. The remedy for this second extreme is surely a historical realism which is prepared to give primary weight to the earliest and fullest evidence rather than to imaginative reconstructions on the basis of later hints.

FAITH AND HISTORY

I want to plead, then, for a historical realism which will allow us to recognise in the Jesus of the New Testament a real-life figure in the context of first-century Palestine, a context which historical research is making constantly more accessible to us.

But, vital as this historical perspective is, it is not the end of the story. For the historical evidence we have been considering points to conclusions which lie outside the area which some modern scholars will allow to be 'historical'. For in the New Testament there is a blend of down-to-earth realism with a frankly 'other-worldly' dimension. Its writers seem to find no difficulty in depicting a central character who was fully a man of his times, and yet whose life and teaching pointed beyond the limited confines of a secular world-view. For them the same man who was hungry, tired, and emotionally upset, who made friends among the more seedy element of the population and enemies among the establishment, who became embroiled in the political power-struggle of occupied Palestine and ended up the loser, one political criminal among others – this same man offered hope, forgiveness of sins, a new life, a new way to the knowledge of God, presented his mission in veiled but unmistakable ways as God's last word, indeed as nothing less than the eschatological coming of God to visit his people, and eventually astounded his followers with the ultimately 'unhistorical' event of a physical resurrection from death.

Many have wished to separate off this 'other-worldly' layer from the more comfortably secular elements in the story of Jesus. But this can be achieved only by doing violence to the New Testament evidence, for the first Christians recognised no such distinction. For them Jesus the wandering 'charismatic' and Jesus the risen Son of God were the same person, the same figure of history. It is this paradoxical Jesus, who is at the same time first-century Jew and Son of God, to whom the historical evidence points. The Jesus known to the earliest Christians was, in the words of one of the earliest Christian confessions,[7] 'descended from David according to the flesh, and designated Son of God in power . . . by his resurrection from the dead' (Romans 1:3–4). The historical records offer us no other.

In the introductory chapter I mentioned that 'historical' evidence of the sort we have been considering is not the only evidence for Jesus. There is also the evidence of Christian faith and experience, both throughout history and today.

For some readers of this book that is the evidence that really matters, and the researches and arguments of the historians carry little weight. But I hope that this book has shown them that historical study of Jesus is a friend rather than an enemy, when it is conducted with a due openness to the full range of the evidence, and indeed that it should enrich rather than threaten their knowledge of Jesus.

For other readers, even to speak of the evidence of faith and experience is to retreat from the hard-won independence of modern man, with his scientific understanding of his world, into the dark ages of superstition and dogma. But our study has brought us to the point where the historical evidence itself points beyond merely secular horizons to a less limited concept of reality, because it has confronted us with a man in history who only makes historical sense in the context of a God-sized universe.

But that is the subject for another book. Our aim here has been more limited: to try to sift through the claims and counter-claims of historians, apologists and sceptics, and to establish a responsible historical basis for our assessment of the man who, on any showing, has affected the course of history more than anyone else who ever lived.

Notes

In these notes certain books which are frequently referred to are abbreviated as follows:

Bruce, *JCOONT*	F. F. Bruce, *Jesus and Christian Origins Outside the New Testament* (London: Hodder, [2]1984).
Finegan, *Archeology*	J. Finegan, *The Archeology of the New Testament* (Princeton University Press, 1969).
Finegan, *Hidden Records*	J. Finegan, *Hidden Records of the Life of Jesus* (Philadelphia: Pilgrim Press, 1969).
Gospel Perspectives	R. T. France & D. Wenham (eds), *Gospel Perspectives: Studies of History and Tradition in the Four Gospels* (Sheffield: JSOT Press, 1980–1985); five volumes to date, one further volume in preparation.
Hennecke	E. Hennecke (ed), *New Testament Apocrypha, vol. 1: Gospels and Related Writings* (ET, London: SCM Press, 1963).
Jeremias, *Unknown Sayings*	J. Jeremias, *Unknown Sayings of Jesus* (ET, London: SPCK, 1957).
Meyers & Strange	E. M. Meyers & J. F. Strange, *Archaeology, the Rabbis and Early Christianity* (London: SCM Press, 1981).
Schürer	E. Schürer, *The History of the Jewish People in the Age of Jesus Christ*, new English edition, ed. G. Vermes, F. Millar & M. Black (Edinburgh: T. & T. Clark, vol. 1, 1973; vol. 2, 1979; vol. 3 awaited).
Wilkinson	J. Wilkinson, *Jerusalem as Jesus Knew It: Archaeology as Evidence* (London: Thames & Hudson, 1978).

Introduction
1. For a brief account of reasons for accepting this reading see B. M. Metzger, *A Textual Commentary on the Greek New Testament*

(London/New York: United Bible Societies, 1971) pp. 67–68. More fully D. P. Senior, *The Passion Narrative according to Matthew* (Leuven University Press, 1975) pp. 238–240.

2. G. A. Wells, *The Jesus of the Early Christians* (London: Pemberton, 1971); *Did Jesus Exist?* (London: Pemberton, 1975); *The Historical Evidence for Jesus* (New York: Prometheus, 1982).

3. J. M. Allegro, *The Sacred Mushroom and the Cross* (London: Hodder & Stoughton, 1970). The scornful rejection of Allegro's theory by Wells, *The Historical Evidence for Jesus*, pp. 220–223, makes interesting reading. More recently Allegro, who had earlier suggested an Essene origin for Christianity (see note 57 on p. 176), has developed a more elaborate argument to the effect that former members of the Qumran sect, who already saw their 'Teacher of Righteousness' in terms of a Joshua/Jesus mythology based on the Old Testament Joshua, son of Nun, developed in the Christian gospels a story of a 'Jesus' in the first century AD; *The Dead Sea Scrolls and the Christian Myth* (1979; Rev. Ed. Buffalo NY: Prometheus, 1984).

4. See especially the works of S. G. F. Brandon, *The Fall of Jerusalem and the Christian Church* (London: SPCK, 1951); *The Trial of Jesus of Nazareth* (London: Batsford, 1968); and especially *Jesus and the Zealots* (Manchester University Press, 1967). Cf. also Joel Carmichael, *The Death of Jesus* (London: Gollancz, 1963).

5. H. J. Schonfield, *The Passover Plot* (London: Hutchinson, 1965).

6. M. Smith, *Jesus the Magician* (London: Gollancz, 1978). The book was described by Hugh Trevor-Roper, in a phrase which was meant to be commendatory, as a 'stimulating work of detection and scholarship'. On Smith's 'new evidence' for Jesus see below pp. 80–81. See also a less scholarly and more fanciful work by Desmond Stewart, *The Foreigner* (London: Hamish Hamilton, 1981), an extraordinary farrago of speculative inferences from odd bits of historical information, purporting to show Jesus as an Egyptian practitioner of necromantic initiatory rites.

7. M. Baigent, R. Leigh & H. Lincoln, *The Holy Blood and the Holy Grail* (London: Jonathan Cape, 1982).

8. See e.g. the remarks of J. A. T. Robinson, *Can We Trust the New Testament?* (London: Mowbray, 1977) pp. 21–25, and the famous strictures of C. S. Lewis on New Testament critics in *Fernseed and Elephants* (London: Collins, 1975) pp. 104–125.

9. A book related to the series by Ian Wilson, *Jesus: the Evidence* (London: Weidenfeld & Nicolson, 1984) gives a rough impression of the nature of the programmes, though its author was in fact very critical of the more radical approach to the assessment of the evidence which was adopted in the programmes; the book itself gives a less disturbing impression than many received from the programmes as they were screened.

10. I did in fact make an attempt at such a portrait in my book, *The Man*

They Crucified: a Portrait of Jesus (Leicester: IVP, 1975). This book discusses the evidence on which that attempt was based.

Chapter 1 Non-Christian Evidence

1. Something of the flavour of Roman attitudes towards Jews may be picked up by leafing through Menahem Stern's excellent anthology (with English translations) of *Greek and Latin Authors on Jews and Judaism* (2 volumes; Jerusalem: Israel Academy of Sciences and Humanities, 1976–1980).

2. F. F. Bruce, *Jesus and Christian Origins Outside the New Testament* (London: Hodder, [2]1984), (hereafter abbreviated as *JCOONT*).

3. *Ibid*, pp. 17–18.

4. This is the only reference to Pilatus in surviving pagan literature, but a reasonable account of his character and his period in office as praefectus of Judaea may be pieced together from the Jewish writers, Philo (*Legatio ad Gaium* 299–305) and Josephus (*BJ* II 169–177; *Ant.* XVIII 35, 55–64, 85–89, 177).

5. Wells, *The Historical Evidence for Jesus*, pp. 16–17, largely repeating his earlier arguments in *Did Jesus Exist?*, pp. 13–15.

6. For the text of the relevant part of the letter, and discussion of its significance, see J. Blinzler, *The Trial of Jesus* (Cork: Mercier Press, 1959) pp. 34–38; Bruce, *JCOONT*, pp. 30–31.

7. Blinzler, *Trial of Jesus*, pp. 35–36 argues for a date soon after AD 73.

8. C. H. H. Scobie, *John the Baptist* (London: SCM Press, 1964) pp. 187–202, discusses the evidence for this continuing 'Baptist sect'.

9. Josephus *Ant.* XVIII 116–119.

10. For further Christian interpolations found in the Slavonic version of Josephus, see Bruce, *JCOONT*, chapter 3. These include a much expanded version of the *Testimonium Flavianum*, inserted this time in Book II of the *Jewish War*.

11. Contrast the greatly embellished account of James' death quoted by Eusebius, *HE* II xxiii 4–18 from the second-century Christian writer Hegesippus. Cf. also Eusebius' own laudatory account, *HE* II xxiii 1–3.

12. Wells, *The Historical Evidence for Jesus*, p. 211, points out that the same phrase occurs in Matthew 1:16, and therefore must be translated 'called' rather than (derogatorily) 'so-called'. But Josephus' usage should be determined from Josephus, not from Matthew. The *Complete Concordance to Flavius Josephus* translates *legomenos* as 'so-called' or 'alleged', and refers as an example to Josephus, *Contra Apionem* II 34, where he speaks of Alexandria as Apion's 'not birthplace, but alleged (birthplace)'. Even if *legomenos* does not necessarily carry this dismissive tone in our passage, it is hardly conceivable that a Christian interpolator could have been content with so non-committal a phrase.

13. Origen, *Comm. in Matt.* X 17.

14. This testimony of Origen is weakened, however, by the observation that there is a parallel passage in Origen, *Contra Celsum* I 47, which makes a similar point, and again quotes the phrase *ho legomenos Christos*, but this time the wording is identical with that of a second alleged account of James' death by Josephus, which Eusebius (*HE* II xxiii 20–24) quotes in full alongside the one which exists in our text of Josephus, *Ant.* XX 197, 199–203. This second account, which does not occur in our text of Josephus, is more explicitly laudatory, calling James 'the righteous' and 'most righteous', and suggesting that his murder was the cause of the destruction of Jerusalem shortly afterwards; it may therefore be a Christian interpolation, even though it too uses the phrase *ho legomenos Christos*. If Origen's comments are, as they seem to be, based on this 'Christian' text, they do not prove the authenticity of *Ant.* XX 200; but the very difference in tone between *Ant.* XX 200 and Eusebius' second text may in itself suggest the authenticity of the former.

15. See the discussion by P. Winter in Schürer, vol. 1, pp. 430–432. Winter appears, however, to be unaware of the second 'Josephus' text quoted by Eusebius, to which I referred in the last note.

16. Wells, *Did Jesus Exist?*, p. 10.

17. Tacitus, *Annals* II 85; Suetonius, *Tiberius* 36.

18. Josephus, *Ant.* XVIII 109–126, with the 'digression' on John in sections 116–119.

19. For a useful survey of views and discussion of the text see P. Winter in Schürer, vol. 1, pp. 428–441.

20. Eusebius, *HE* I xi 7–8 is virtually identical with our MSS of Josephus; *Demonstratio* III v 105 differs in a few words, none of which affect the substance of the account.

21. Josephus, *Ant.* VIII 53; X 237.

22. Josephus, *Ant.* IX 182. *Paradoxos* is also used by Josephus of Moses' miracle of providing water (*Ant.* III 38) and of examples of uncanny foreknowledge (*Ant.* XIII 282; XV 379). There is one similar use in the New Testament (Luke 5:26).

23. *BJ* II 397; III 354; *Ant.* XIV 115.

24. *BJ* II 366, 372, 379, 381, etc.

25. *Ant.* II 306 (locusts!); XIII 430 (the female sex).

26. Bruce, *JCOONT*, p. 39 (quoted with permission).

27. This phrase is added because the following section (65ff) suggests that other causes of trouble have just been mentioned.

28. 'Strange things' depends on a conjecture that 'the truth' (*talēthē*) has replaced an original *taēthē*, 'the unusual'.

29. To see this and the other texts from *Sanhedrin* quoted below in their talmudic context, see I. Epstein (ed), *The Babylonian Talmud* (London: Soncino Press, 18-vol. edition 1961), Seder Nezikin, vol. III. The meaning of a *baraita* is, however, independent of the (later) context.

30. *Sanhedrin* 6:1.
31. This discussion is of death by stoning, but Mishnah *Sanhedrin* 6:4 requires that the body of a man executed by stoning on a charge of blasphemy or idolatry should then be hanged in public.
32. This is the set form of words prescribed in Mishnah *Sanhedrin* 6:1, with the specific offence of Yeshu added.
33. This is, incidentally, an interesting support for the so-called 'Johannine' chronology of the passion, as opposed to the view usually attributed to the synoptic gospels that Jesus died on the day *after* the Passover meal.
34. See however J. A. T. Robinson, *The Priority of John* (London: SCM, 1985) pp. 225–229 for the suggestion that the 'real' trial of Jesus by the Jewish authorities was that recorded in John 11:47–53, so that there was in fact 'a considerable time' for appeal between the verdict (John 11:53) and its implementation.
35. This *baraita* was censored from later editions of the Talmud, and in modern editions appears, if at all, in a footnote. Another version of the story occurs in *Sotah* 47a, but without Jesus' name in the main MSS – he is referred to as 'a disciple' (of Rabbi Joshua).
36. *Sanhedrin* 10:2.
37. This word can mean either an 'inn' (which is presumably what Joshua meant) or a 'female innkeeper' (which is how Jesus is alleged to have understood it, hence Joshua's rebuke of his misguided thoughts).
38. So E. Bammel, *NTS* 13 (1966/7) pp. 321–322. My colleague Jean-Marc Heimerdinger suggests a different explanation, that Jesus' alleged misunderstanding reflects the Rabbinic criticism of Christianity as having too great an interest in women, who received in the Christian community a prominence which scandalised orthodox Rabbinic Jews. See also R. T. Herford, *Christianity in Talmud and Midrash* (London: Williams & Norgate, 1903) p. 53.
39. The reference is to the massacres of his Jewish opponents by Alexander Jannaeus (103–76 BC); Josephus, *Ant.* XIII 383, confirms that some of them fled the country. As far as I know only one writer has used this connection to argue that Jesus actually did live about 100 BC! (G. R. S. Mead, *Did Jesus Live 100 BC?* [London: Theosophical Publishing Society, 1903].)
40. D. R. Catchpole, *The Trial of Jesus* (Leiden: Brill, 1971) pp. 1–4, draws attention to this as a survival of an earlier and more positive view of Jesus than that found in most talmudic passages.
41. The accusation that Jesus brought his magical arts from Egypt can be traced back at least to the end of the first century AD, in the words of Eliezer ben Hyrcanus, recorded in *Shabbath* 104b, if it is accepted that Ben Stada was a pseudonym for Jesus; on this identification see below pp. 37–38.
42. For English text see J. Neusner (ed), *The Tosefta*, vol. V, Qodoshim (New York: KTAV, 1979) pp. 74–75 (quoted with permission).

43. A fuller account in Babylonian Talmud *Abodah Zarah* 16b–17a tells us what that teaching was. It bears no relation to any known saying of Jesus. Most MSS of the Talmud do not include the name of Jesus in this version.
44. Origen *Contra Celsum* I 32.
45. A similar passage occurs in the uncensored text of *Shabbath* 104b, following the mention of Ben Stada's bringing his magic from Egypt; see above n. 41.
46. R. T. Herford, *Christianity in Talmud and Midrash*, pp. 35–41, accepts without reservation the identification of Ben Stada with Jesus. D. R. Catchpole, *Trial of Jesus*, pp. 35, 44–47, 61–64, accepts it more guardedly.
47. For other, more tenuous, 'evidence' see Bruce, *JCOONT*, pp. 58–65, and much more fully Herford, *Christianity in Talmud and Midrash*, *passim*, especially the summary on pp. 344–360.
48. Something of the flavour of this later material may be discerned from E. Bammel's article on 'Christian Origins in Jewish Traditions', *NTS* 13 (1966/7) pp. 317–335, and from W. Horbury, 'The Trial of Jesus in Jewish Tradition', in E. Bammel (ed), *The Trial of Jesus* (London: SCM Press, 1970) pp. 103–121. See further, both for the *Toledoth* and for a broader range of possible talmudic references to Jesus, J. Jocz, *The Jewish People and Jesus Christ* (London: SPCK, 1949) pp. 59–65.
49. Wells, *Did Jesus Exist?*, p. 12.
50. E.g. Josephus does not mention any Jew called Chrestus.
51. Tertullian, *Apol.* 3. Greek-speaking Christian apologists often exploited the similarity in sound, e.g. Justin, *Apol.* I 4; Clement of Alexandria, *Strom.* II 4.
52. An amusing offshoot of this discussion is the assertion of D. Stewart, *The Foreigner*, pp. 25, 77–78, that Chrestus was in fact a nickname which Jesus acquired during his alleged youth in Alexandria. It was subsequent corruption of this name which led to his being called 'Christ'! This odd theory is explicitly based on the Suetonius passage; and yet if, as Stewart is arguing, Chrestus in this passage is the real name of the person concerned, and not a mistake for Christus, there is absolutely no reason to interpret the passage as having anything to do with Jesus in the first place!
53. This last comment presumably refers to popular allegations that Christians indulged in cannibalism, an inference easily drawn from references to eating and drinking Christ's body and blood.
54. This is a summary of a long letter, which is entirely devoted to the subject of Christianity: Pliny, *Ep.* X 96; X 97 is Trajan's reply.
55. There is by now a voluminous and constantly growing literature on Qumran. The best reasonably up-to-date overview of the discussion, with useful bibliographies for further study, is G. Vermes, *The Dead Sea Scrolls: Qumran in Perspective* (London: Collins, 1977). The texts themselves are most conveniently assembled in English translation in

the same author's *The Dead Sea Scrolls in English* (Harmondsworth: Penguin, [2]1975).

56. So J. L. Teicher in *JJS* 2 (1951) pp. 67–99, and further articles in issues of the same journal over the following few years.

57. So e.g. A. Dupont-Sommer, *The Essene Writings from Qumran* (ET, Oxford: Blackwell, [2]1961) especially pp. 368–378, 395–397; J. M. Allegro, *The Dead Sea Scrolls* (Harmondsworth: Penguin, 1956) pp. 155–162. (Allegro's sacred mushroom theory came later!)

58. This link is explored by W. H. Brownlee in K. Stendahl (ed), *The Scrolls and the New Testament* (London: SCM Press, 1958) pp. 33–53.

59. A stimulating earlier study was chapter 2 of G. Vermes, *Jesus the Jew* (London: Collins, 1973). The major treatment is S. Freyne, *Galilee from Alexander the Great to Hadrian* (Wilmington: Glazier, 1980). A good survey of recent discussion is Meyers & Strange, pp. 31–47; they propose a further sharp distinction between Upper and Lower Galilee.

60. A useful summary of the question of languages in first-century Palestine is given by P. E. Hughes in R. N. Longenecker & M. C. Tenney (eds), *New Dimensions in New Testament Study* (Grand Rapids: Zondervan, 1974) pp. 127–143. More fully, and more technically, see J. A. Fitzmyer, 'The Languages of Palestine in the First Century', *CBQ* 30 (1972) pp. 501–531; C. Rabin, 'Hebrew and Aramaic in the First Century', in S. Safrai & M. Stern (eds), *Compendia Rerum Iudaicarum ad Novum Testamentum*, I/2 (Assen: Van Gorcum, 1976) pp. 1007–1039. Meyers & Strange, pp. 62–91, provide a more up-to-date survey of the relevant archaeological data. See further below pp. 145–147.

61. G. Theissen, *Miracle Stories of the Early Christian Tradition* (ET, Edinburgh: T. & T. Clark, 1983) p. 266. Part Three of Theissen's book (pp. 231–302) contains many fascinating details of ancient attitudes to miracles and miracle-workers, collected as a background to understanding the sociological and religious function of the miracle-stories in the gospels.

62. Suetonius, *Vespasian* 23.4.

63. So both Suetonius, *Vespasian* 7.2–3 and Tacitus, *Histories* IV 81.

64. Theissen, *Miracle Stories*, pp. 269–275.

65. The life is published in two volumes of the Loeb Classical Library. For a more painless acquaintance with it, the reader is recommended to use pp. 259–296 of D. L. Dungan & D. R. Cartlidge, *Sourcebook of Texts for the Comparative Study of the Gospels* (Missoula: Society of Biblical Literature, [3]1973). The *Sourcebook* as a whole is a valuable collection of extracts from ancient literature, pagan, Jewish and Christian, which allow us to read the gospels in the wider literary context in which they were written.

66. Vermes, *Jesus the Jew*, pp. 69–78. For a fuller account of Hanina ben Dosa see Vermes' articles in *JJS* 23 (1972) pp. 28–50 and 24 (1973) pp. 51–64.

67. *Ant.* VIII 46–48; cf. *BJ* VII 185. For further details of the Jewish theory and practice of exorcism see G. Vermes, *Jesus the Jew*, pp. 63–69.
68. *BJ* VII 252–253. For the relations of Sicarii and Zealots, and the differing uses of terms, see Schürer, vol. 2, pp. 598–606, with full references to recent discussion.
69. So especially S. G. F. Brandon, *Jesus and the Zealots* (Manchester University Press, 1967).
70. So, in various works, M. Hengel; see especially his *Was Jesus a Revolutionist?* and *Victory over Violence* (ET, Philadelphia: Fortress Press, 1971 and 1973 respectively). There is a very full discussion of many related issues in the symposium E. Bammel & C. F. D. Moule (eds), *Jesus and the Politics of His Day* (Cambridge University Press, 1984). 'The Zealots and Jesus', the first essay in that volume, by J. P. M. Sweet, gives a useful brief summary and critique of Brandon's view; subsequent essays discuss in detail the key themes and passages on which his thesis was based.
71. Lewis, *Fernseed and Elephants*, p. 111.
72. S. Sandmel, 'Parallelomania', *JBL* 81 (1962) pp. 1–13.
73. *Ibid*, p. 4.
74. This is the title of the first main chapter of E. Schweizer, *Jesus* (ET, London: SCM Press, 1971).

Chapter 2　Christian Evidence outside the New Testament
1. A late first-century date seems probable for the First Letter of Clement, and is claimed with some plausibility for the Epistle of Barnabas and for at least part of the Didache by some scholars.
2. For full text and comments see e.g. Finegan, *Hidden Records*, pp. 178–186; Bruce, *JCOONT*, pp. 160–164; R. M. Grant & D. N. Freedman, *The Secret Sayings of Jesus* (London: Collins, 1960) pp. 52–55.
3. For the texts see Finegan, *Hidden Records*, pp. 187–205; Grant & Freedman, *Secret Sayings*, pp. 44–49; Hennecke, vol. 1, pp. 97–113.
4. The full texts, in English translation, are published in J. M. Robinson (ed), *The Nag Hammadi Library* (Leiden: Brill, 1977; New York: Harper & Row, 1981).
5. The *Decretum Gelasianum*, a list of scores of such works, the authors of which, together with their adherents, are 'to be damned in the inextricable shackles of anathema for ever', was issued probably around the beginning of the sixth century. For the text see Hennecke, vol. 1, pp. 47–49.
6. The attempt by P. Vielhauer in Hennecke, vol. 1, pp. 139–165, to reconstruct the outlines of these as three separate gospels involves a great deal of speculation which would not be accepted by other scholars.
7. This is the title of a book by Elaine Pagels (London: Weidenfeld

& Nicolson, 1980), popularising some of the contents of the Nag Hammadi documents.

8. So especially the 'Gospel of Truth', the Gospel of Thomas, and the Gospel of Philip among the Nag Hammadi treatises.

9. For examples of this type of treatise among the Nag Hammadi documents, see the Apocryphon of James, the Apocryphon of John, the Book of Thomas the Contender, the Sophia of Jesus Christ, and the two Apocalypses of James.

10. Robinson, *The Nag Hammadi Library*, pp. 207–208 (quoted with permission).

11. For a further sampling of this material see the selection presented by Bruce in *JCOONT*, chapter 6. Fuller collections are offered by Hennecke, vol. 1, and by Finegan, *Hidden Records*. A more popular presentation, restricted to the Nag Hammadi material, is Pagels, *The Gnostic Gospels*, though the publisher's claim that 'she shows us how these extraordinary texts compel us to reconsider profoundly the traditional view of the origins and meanings of Christianity' considerably outruns the author's own claims!

12. J. Jeremias, *Unknown Sayings of Jesus* (ET, London: SPCK, 1957, German original 1951). The book was written before most of the Nag Hammadi material was available. The subsequent publication of the Gospel of Thomas in particular provided a literary setting for what, when Jeremias wrote, had been apparently isolated sayings of Jesus in the Oxyrhynchus Papyri.

13. This last saying, discussed by Jeremias, *Unknown Sayings*, pp. 99–100, runs: 'Jesus, on whom be peace, has said, "This world is a bridge. Pass over it. But build not your dwelling there."' The idea reflects the simpler saying in the Gospel of Thomas (no. 42), 'Be like those who pass over (or pass by)'.

14. Jeremias, *Unknown Sayings*, p. 30.

15. For further discussion of this saying see Jeremias, *Unknown Sayings*, pp. 49–53, arguing enthusiastically for its genuineness. Most commentators are more sceptical; see e.g. E. Lohse, *TDNT* VII, pp. 23–24.

16. Tertullian, *De Baptismo* 20.

17. Clement of Alexandria, *Strom.* I 24.

18. Origen, *De Orat.* II 2; XIV 1.

19. G. W. H. Lampe, *A Patristic Greek Lexicon* (Oxford University Press, 1961) p. 1400, lists fifteen quotations of this saying between the second and fifth centuries, and a further thirteen clear allusions to it.

20. For details see Jeremias, *Unknown Sayings*, pp. 89–93, with full discussion. Cyril of Alexandria quoted it as from Paul.

21. Origen, *Comm. in Joh.* XIX 7. Clement of Alexandria, *Strom.* I 28, similarly interprets it with a paraphrase of 1 Thessalonians 5:21: 'Reject some things, but hold on to what is good.'

22. In addition to Jeremias' twenty-one sayings, Finegan, *Hidden Records*,

pp. 123–175, presents and discusses others (fifty in all) deriving from early Christian literature.

23. Origen, *Comm. in Matt.* XV 14.
24. Jeremias, *Unknown Sayings*, pp. 33–36, disagrees and argues from the vividness of a few details, the Palestinian colour, the consistency with Jesus' canonical teaching, and especially the 'moral urgency', that it is an independent version of the story.
25. For the text see Finegan, *Hidden Records*, pp. 226–230; Hennecke, vol. 1, pp. 93–94.
26. Jeremias, *Unknown Sayings*, pp. 36–49.
27. Jerome, *De Viris Illustribus* 2.
28. For full text in English see Hennecke, vol. 1, pp. 374–388.
29. For full text in English see Hennecke, vol. 1, pp. 392–401.
30. Above pp. 60–61.
31. Here and in what follows I am using (with permission) the translation by B. M. Metzger, printed in K. Aland (ed), *Synopsis Quattuor Evangeliorum* (Stuttgart: Württembergische Bibelanstalt, 1963) pp. 517–530. The full text in English may also be found in Robinson, *The Nag Hammadi Library*, pp. 118–130, and, with comments, in Bruce, *JCOONT*, chapter 7, and in Grant & Freedman, *The Secret Sayings of Jesus*, pp. 112–186.
32. See p. 64.
33. Clement of Alexandria, *Strom.* II 9, in abbreviated form; it is quoted in full in *Strom.* V 14, but there without the attribution to the Gospel according to the Hebrews.
34. Origen, *Hom. in Jer.* XX 3 (Latin version).
35. Jeremias, *Unknown Sayings*, pp. 54–56.
36. See above p. 68.
37. Eusebius, *HE* VI 12, tells the story.
38. For the text in English see e.g. Bruce, *JCOONT*, pp. 88–92; Hennecke, vol. 1, pp. 183–187.
39. The caption writer in Wilson, *Jesus: the Evidence*, has again outrun the facts when he states (p. 25) that Morton Smith 'discovered the "secret" version of the gospel of Mark at the desert monastery of Mar Saba'. What Smith in fact discovered was a copy of a letter purporting to quote from such a gospel.
40. M. Smith, *Clement of Alexandria and a Secret Gospel of Mark* (Harvard University Press, 1973).
41. M. Smith, *The Secret Gospel* (New York: Harper & Row, 1973; London: Gollancz, 1974).
42. M. Smith, *Jesus the Magician* (London: Gollancz, 1978).
43. That such 'adaptations' of the canonical gospels were in fact current may be illustrated from Epiphanius' comments on the 'Hebrew Gospel' used by the Ebionites, which he describes as a 'forged and mutilated' version of the Gospel of Matthew. See Hennecke, vol. 1, p. 156.

44. For details see F. F. Bruce, *The 'Secret' Gospel of Mark* (London: Athlone Press, 1974) pp. 12–16. Bruce's booklet provides altogether a valuable critical assessment of Smith's claims.
45. So H. Montefiore & H. E. W. Turner, *Thomas and the Evangelists* (London: SCM Press, 1962) pp. 15–16.
46. For an imaginative example of this sort of approach, partly based on Smith's work, see Stewart, *The Foreigner*, especially chapters 15 and 20. As an example of the extremes to which uncontrolled speculation can go on the basis of a few unconnected hints and in defiance of the vast mass of historical evidence, Stewart's book would be hard to beat.
47. Above pp. 68, 77–78.
48. See e.g. the reconstructions noted above on pp. 12–14.

Chapter 3 The Evidence of the New Testament

1. For a full study of 'the Jesus tradition outside the gospels' see the fifth volume of *Gospel Perspectives* (1985).
2. See G. R. Beasley-Murray, *The Book of Revelation* (New Century Bible. London: Oliphants, 1974) pp. 39ff.
3. See above pp. 65–66.
4. See e.g. the table of parallels in P. H. Davids, *The Epistle of James* (New International Greek Testament Commentary. Exeter: Paternoster, 1982) pp. 47–49 and his more recent essay 'James and Jesus' in *Gospel Perspectives*, vol. 5, pp. 63–84.
5. Wells, *The Historical Evidence for Jesus*, p. 22.
6. Wells' view of Paul is set out *ibid.*, pp. 22–45.
7. See most commentaries on 2 Corinthians. Particularly full and helpful here is P. E. Hughes, *Paul's Second Letter to the Corinthians* (New London Commentary. London: Marshall, Morgan & Scott, 1962) pp. 197–201.
8. C. K. Barrett, *A Commentary on the First Epistle to the Corinthians* (Black's New Testament Commentary. London: A. & C. Black, [2]1971) pp. 264–266, helpfully discusses this phrase, concluding that it speaks not of a direct, unmediated revelation, but of a historical tradition which originated with 'the Lord' (i.e. Jesus) as the first link in the chain.
9. Even Wells, *The Historical Evidence for Jesus* p. 28, speaks here of Paul reproducing a 'tradition'.
10. See further the very full study by J. Jeremias, *The Eucharistic Words of Jesus* (ET, London: SCM Press, 1966). Pages 101–105 particularly focus on 1 Corinthians 11:23–25 as evidence for an independent historical tradition, especially when studied alongside 1 Corinthians 15:1ff.
11. It is interesting that Wells, *The Historical Evidence for Jesus* pp. 24–25, is reduced to eliminating this passage as a later interpolation into Paul's letter, a convenient speculation for which there is no basis in the textual evidence.

12. Again, most commentaries will spell out the case. For Romans 1:3–4 see also P. Beasley-Murray, 'Romans 1:3f: An early confession of faith in the lordship of Jesus', in *Tyn B* 31 (1980) pp. 147–154. For Philippians 2:6–11, most fully R. P. Martin, *Carmen Christi* (Cambridge University Press, 1967; revised edition, Grand Rapids: Eerdmans, 1983).

13. See above pp. 65–66. Jeremias discusses this saying in *Unknown Sayings*, pp. 64–67.

14. E. Best, *The First and Second Epistles to the Thessalonians* (Black's New Testament Commentary. London: A. & C. Black, 1972) pp. 189–193, offers a helpful discussion of alternative views of the origin of this saying, and concludes that its origin in Christian prophecy is 'by far the most probable'. A similar conclusion is reached by D. E. Aune, *Prophecy in Early Christianity and the Ancient Mediterranean World* (Grand Rapids: Eerdmans, 1983) pp. 253–256.

15. For an interesting discussion of Paul's argument in 1 Corinthians 7 from the point of view of Rabbinic ideas of authority see B. Gerhardsson, *Memory and Manuscript* (Uppsala, 1961), pp. 311–314.

16. G. N. Stanton, *Jesus of Nazareth in New Testament Preaching* (Cambridge University Press, 1974) p. 115. The whole chapter on Paul (pp. 86–116) repays study in this connection.

17. For an excellent fuller account, but still designed for the reader who is not a specialist in this area, see I. H. Marshall, *I Believe in the Historical Jesus* (London: Hodder & Stoughton, 1977), especially chapter 6 for the development of this view. I have written a briefer account and critique in 'The Authenticity of the Sayings of Jesus', an essay in C. Brown (ed), *History, Criticism and Faith* (Leicester: IVP, 1976) pp. 101–143. A more ambitious attempt to address this question is the Gospels Project sponsored by Tyndale House, Cambridge, from which has originated the series *Gospel Perspectives*; a more popular book by C. L. Blomberg, setting out the results of the Project, is expected soon from IVP, Leicester.

18. For a brief introduction to the idea of 'myth' in the New Testament see F. F. Bruce, 'Myth and History' in Brown, *History, Criticism and Faith*, pp. 79–99.

19. This point has been argued, with reference to biographical writing in the Graeco-Roman world, by C. H. Talbert, *What is a Gospel?* (London: SPCK, 1978). There are serious weaknesses in Talbert's work, as D. E. Aune has pointed out at length in *Gospel Perspectives*, vol. 2, pp. 9–60, but the comparative material he has collected does suffice to show that Bultmann's dictum that the gospels are not biographies was more appropriate to modern than to ancient 'biography'.

20. R. Bultmann, *The History of the Synoptic Tradition* (ET, Oxford: Blackwell, 1963) pp. 6–7.

21. Among several recent discussions see especially D. Hill, *New Testament Prophecy* (London: Marshall, Morgan & Scott, 1979) and M. E.

Boring, *Sayings of the Risen Jesus* (Cambridge University Press, 1982). Boring advocates the idea of prophets as originators of 'sayings of Jesus', while Hill opposes it. Most recently Aune, *Prophecy in Early Christianity*, has judged Boring's case not proven, and concludes that it is 'unlikely that many oracles of the risen Lord became assimilated to sayings of the historical Jesus' (p. 245, summarising the discussion of pp. 233ff).

22. See above p. 92 for this distinction in Paul, and see further my article in Brown, *History, Criticism and Faith*, pp. 123–126.

23. This approach is clearly seen in M. D. Goulder, *Midrash and Lection in Matthew* (London: SPCK, 1974) and J. Drury, *Tradition and Design in Luke's Gospel* (London: Darton, Longman & Todd, 1976). More popularly, it is presented by H. J. Richards, *The First Christmas* (London: Collins, 1973), and is apparently welcomed by D. Winter, *The Search for the Real Jesus* (London: Hodder & Stoughton, 1982) p. 41.

24. The whole of vol. 3 of *Gospel Perspectives* is devoted to this question of 'midrash'; on pp. 289–299 of that volume I have tried to draw out some conclusions which throw doubt on the whole approach to the gospels as 'midrash'. With special reference to the stories of Matthew 1–2 see further my essay 'Scripture, Tradition and History in the Infancy Narratives of Matthew' in *Gospel Perspectives*, vol. 2, pp. 239–266.

25. G. Bornkamm, *Jesus of Nazareth* (ET, London: Hodder & Stoughton, 1960). In fairness it should be pointed out that this sentence, picked out by the publishers for display on the cover, is only one half of a statement which continues, 'But no one should despise the help of historical research to illumine the truth with which each of us should be concerned.'

26. Wells, *The Historical Evidence for Jesus*, pp. 10–11 and 107–113.

27. N. Perrin, *Rediscovering the Teaching of Jesus* (London: SCM Press, 1967) p. 24.

28. This view was spelled out especially in M. Kähler's book published in 1892, whose English title is *The So-called Historical Jesus and the Historic, Biblical Christ* (Philadelphia: Fortress Press, 1964). This book, and the terminology of its title, has been extremely influential in twentieth-century scholarship.

29. This view is succinctly expressed, for instance, by N. Perrin, *Rediscovering*, p. 39. For a clear statement to the contrary see J. Jeremias, *New Testament Theology, vol. 1: The Proclamation of Jesus* (ET, London: SCM Press, 1971) p. 37.

30. This is the term proposed by N. Perrin, *Rediscovering*, p. 39, though the criterion had earlier been explicitly set out and operated by Bultmann (e.g. *The History of the Synoptic Tradition*, p. 205) and those who followed his approach to gospel criticism.

31. N. Perrin, *Rediscovering*, p. 43.

32. Many similar critical assessments of the 'criteria of authenticity'

approach have been published. I have discussed the issue at more length in Brown, *History, Criticism and Faith*, pp. 107–117. One of the fullest discussions is by R. H. Stein, 'The "criteria" for Authenticity', *Gospel Perspectives*, vol. 1, pp. 225–263.

33. H. Riesenfeld, *The Gospel Tradition and its Beginnings* (London: Mowbray, 1957); also published in *Studia Evangelica* I (TU 73. Berlin: Akademie-Verlag, 1958) pp. 43–65, and in H. Riesenfeld, *The Gospel Tradition* (Oxford: Blackwell, 1970) pp. 1–29.

34. The main work is B. Gerhardsson, *Memory and Manuscript* (Uppsala, 1961), with a supplementary discussion in *Tradition and Transmission in Early Christianity* (Lund: Gleerup, 1964), and a more popular presentation in *The Origins of the Gospel Traditions* (ET, London: SCM Press, 1979).

35. Mishnah *Aboth* 2:8.

36. For a careful assessment of Gerhardsson's thesis in the light of subsequent debate see P. H. Davids 'The Gospels and Jewish Tradition: Twenty Years after Gerhardsson' in *Gospel Perspectives*, vol. 1, pp. 75–99.

37. Riesner's dissertation, *Jesus als Lehrer: eine Untersuchung zum Ursprung der Evangelien-Überlieferung* (Tübingen: Mohr, 1981) is unfortunately not yet available in English. An article distilling some of the results of his research is in *Gospel Perspectives*, vol. 1, pp. 209–233, also in German.

38. R. Riesner, *Jesus als Lehrer*, p. 502 (my translation).

39. K. E. Bailey is well known for his studies of the Lucan parables in terms of their setting in Middle Eastern culture. See especially his *Poet and Peasant* and *Through Peasant Eyes*, now published in a combined edition (Grand Rapids: Eerdmans, 1976, 1980; combined edition 1983). The work referred to in this paragraph is written up in an as yet unpublished paper entitled 'Informal, Controlled Oral Tradition and the Synoptic Gospels'.

40. The point is delightfully illustrated by the story of the 'translation machine' which rendered word-for-word into Japanese the sentence 'The spirit is willing but the flesh is weak'; the resultant sentence was then translated back into English as 'There is some good whisky, but the roast beef is mediocre'. (J. P. Louw, *Semantics of New Testament Greek* [Philadelphia: Fortress Press, 1982] p. 71.)

41. This quotation is drawn from a helpful summary of John's approach by G. E. Ladd, *The New Testament and Criticism* (London: Hodder & Stoughton, 1970) p. 137. Ladd continues, 'John's mind became saturated with the remembered teachings of Jesus so that the form of Jesus' teaching also became adapted in his own mind to John's own idiom, until at last a single style resulted in which the form of Jesus' words and the idiom of John himself are merged.'

42. The so-called 'Augustinian' view, proposing the order Matthew – Mark – Luke, was argued by B. C. Butler, *The Originality of St*

Matthew (Cambridge University Press, 1951). Recently attention has been focused more on the 'Griesbach Hypothesis', proposing the order Matthew – Luke – Mark; see especially W. R. Farmer, *The Synoptic Problem* (Dillsboro: Western North Carolina Press, ²1976); B. Orchard, *Matthew, Luke and Mark* (Manchester: Koinonia Press, 1976).

43. So especially J. M. Rist, *On the Independence of Matthew and Mark* (Cambridge University Press, 1978).

44. J. A. T. Robinson, *Redating the New Testament* (London: SCM Press, 1976).

45. This scheme is summarised by Robinson, *ibid*, p. 107, but is spelled out more fully on pp. 93–117.

46. Robinson, *ibid*, pp. 86–92 surveys earlier views, especially the important 'conversion' of the liberal scholar Adolf von Harnack to acceptance of a date in the early sixties. See further F. F. Bruce, *The Acts of the Apostles* (London: Tyndale Press, 1951) pp. 10–14 for a clear outline of the arguments for an early date.

47. For a recent detailed argument for a date for Matthew in the early sixties see R. H. Gundry, *Matthew: a Commentary on his Literary and Theological Art* (Grand Rapids: Eerdmans, 1982) pp. 599–609.

48. See however M. Hengel, *Studies in the Gospel of Mark* (ET, London: SCM, 1985) pp. 64–84, for an argument that the titles go back to the first century, and were associated with the gospels from their origin.

49. These and other grounds of canonicity are usefully discussed by F. F. Bruce, 'New Light on the Origins of the New Testament Canon' in Longenecker & Tenney, *New Dimensions in New Testament Study*, pp. 3–18.

50. Marcion, a Gnostic teacher about the middle of the second century, accepted only Luke's gospel – and radically expurgated even that in order to support his views! An obscure group in Asia Minor, the 'Alogi', finding that the gospel of John was favoured by Gnostics, attributed its authorship to the Gnostic Cerinthus.

51. Irenaeus, *Adv. Haer.* III 11.8.

52. Most commentaries on the gospels will include in their introductions an adequate statement of the evangelist's aims and methods. In addition, attention should be drawn to a useful series of books published by the Paternoster Press, which give a fuller discussion: I. H. Marshall, *Luke, Historian and Theologian* (1970); R. P. Martin, *Mark, Evangelist and Theologian* (1972); S. S. Smalley, *John, Evangelist and Interpreter* (1978). The volume on Matthew is still awaited.

53. For a full account of Ramsay's work see W. W. Gasque, *Sir William M. Ramsay: Archaeologist and New Testament Scholar* (Grand Rapids: Baker, 1966). A brief summary may be found in W. W. Gasque, *A History of the Criticism of the Acts of the Apostles* (Tübingen: Mohr, 1975) pp. 136–142. Some of the data which formed the basis of

Ramsay's conclusions are set out more popularly in F. F. Bruce, *The New Testament Documents* (Leicester: IVP, [5]1960) pp. 80–92.

54. So especially the classic account of the problem in Schürer, vol. 1, pp. 399–427.

55. I. H. Marshall, *The Gospel of Luke* (New International Greek Testament Commentary. Exeter: Paternoster, 1978) p. 104. Marshall's commentary, pp. 99–104 provides a careful discussion of the problems and of proposed solutions.

56. This more recent sceptical approach to Luke has been focused on the work of H. Conzelmann and E. Haenchen. It is critically examined by I. H. Marshall in *Luke, Historian and Theologian* (especially pp. 77–88 on Conzelmann) and M. Hengel, *Acts and the History of Earliest Christianity* (ET, London: SCM Press, 1979).

57. C. J. Hemer, 'Luke the Historian' in *BJRL* 60 (1977/8) p. 50.

58. I have explored this argument in two articles: 'The Formula-Quotations of Matthew 2 and the Problem of Communication', *NTS* 27 (1980/81) pp. 233–251; 'Herod and the Children of Bethlehem', *Nov T* 21 (1979) pp. 98–120.

59. See further my discussion in a paper entitled 'Scripture, Tradition and History in the Infancy Narratives of Matthew', *Gospel Perspectives*, vol. 2, pp. 239–266.

60. C. H. Dodd, *Historical Tradition in the Fourth Gospel* (Cambridge University Press, 1963).

61. The phrase is derived from the title of an influential paper by J. A. T. Robinson in 1957. For an account of this 'new look' see chapter 1 of Smalley, *John, Evangelist and Interpreter*.

62. Smalley, *ibid*, pp. 38–39. The move towards a renewed confidence in the historical value of John has found its fullest expression in the recent posthumous work of J. A. T. Robinson, *The Priority of John* (London: SCM, 1985), in which he argues not that John's gospel was the first to be written, but that it should have 'procedural priority', in that its account comes from closest to source.

63. The exact form of the name varies in different Greek MSS; 'Bethzatha' is perhaps the better attested form, but the traditional English version 'Bethesda' also has wide and early support.

64. For the evidence see Wilkinson, pp. 95–104, and for a slightly different account which no less strongly supports John's reliability see Robinson, *The Priority of John*, pp. 54–59. See further below pp. 148–149.

65. For all these points see F. F. Bruce, 'The Trial of Jesus in the Fourth Gospel', *Gospel Perspectives*, vol. 1, pp. 7–20. Bruce draws also on the important study by the Roman historian A. N. Sherwin-White, *Roman Society and Roman Law in the New Testament* (Oxford University Press, 1963); see especially pp. 35–44 on the question of the capital jurisdiction of the Sanhedrin.

66. See above pp. 116–117.

67. The relevant facts and arguments are succinctly set out by Metzger, *Textual Commentary* (London/New York: United Bible Societies, 1971), pp. 122–126.
68. Notably in recent years W. R. Farmer, *The Last Twelve Verses of Mark* (Cambridge University Press, 1974).
69. The evidence is again suitably set out by Metzger, *Textual Commentary*, pp. 219–222.
70. Above pp. 68–72.
71. See above p. 11.
72. B. M. Metzger, *Textual Commentary*, offers a convenient summary of the evidence available and of the accepted principles and methods of textual criticism (pp. xiii–xxxi), as well as an assessment of all the textual variants selected for mention in the UBS Greek text. An informed understanding of New Testament textual criticism necessarily requires at least a rudimentary acquaintance with Greek; given that, a very attractive introduction to the subject is offered by J. Finegan, *Encountering New Testament Manuscripts* (London: SPCK, 1975). A clear, practical student's guide to the subject is J. H. Greenlee, *Introduction to New Testament Textual Criticism* (Grand Rapids: Eerdmans, 1964). The most valuable fuller account is B. M. Metzger, *The Text of the New Testament* (Oxford University Press, [2]1968).

Chapter 4 The Evidence of Archaeology
1. Among the many books which deal with the subjects covered in this chapter, four may be singled out for mention. R. K. Harrison, *Archaeology of the New Testament* (London: Hodder & Stoughton, 1964), while now out of date in some areas, offers a clear, basic collection of relevant evidence. Much fuller and restricted to the Palestinian background of the life of Jesus, is Finegan, *The Archeology of the New Testament* (Princeton University Press, 1969), – though it should be noted that much of the contents is not strictly 'archaeological', but rather a tourist guide to Palestinian sites. Meyers & Strange is more up to date, though more limited in its coverage; its deliberate bringing together of Jewish and Christian interests is valuable for perspective. Finally, Wilkinson is a very full but not over-technical study of great value to the student of the gospels.
2. This section draws in part on the evidence assembled in Meyers & Strange, pp. 48–61, and in part on Wilkinson.
3. It is mentioned in a late third-century inscription from Caesarea; see Finegan, *Archeology*, p. 29. Literary sources do not mention it for much longer – it even fails to appear in the Talmud.
4. Above pp. 46–49.
5. Above p. 50.
6. See N. Avigad, *IEJ* 12 (1962) pp. 9–12.
7. The evidence is summarised in Meyers & Strange, p. 65.

8. For the Theodotus inscription see Meyers & Strange, pp. 82–83; for the Hebrew and Aramaic inscriptions, *ibid*, pp. 69, 76–77.
9. For a full survey see Meyers & Strange, pp. 62–91.
10. See Finegan, *Archeology*, p. 80.
11. See above pp. 21–33.
12. For text and discussion see F. F. Bruce, *New Testament History* (London: Nelson, 1969) pp. 284–286.
13. For these and other details see further Wilkinson, pp. 27–30.
14. Above pp. 131–132.
15. See further J. A. T. Robinson, *The Priority of John*, pp. 57–59, for evidence of spring water in the area in ancient times.
16. For fuller details see Finegan, *Archeology*, pp. 142–147, as well as the discussion by Wilkinson, pp. 95–104.
17. In Mark 12:41, however, we find him by the 'treasury', which was in the 'Court of the Women', the first of the inner courts entered from the Court of the Gentiles.
18. Babylonian Talmud, *Baba Bathra* 4a.
19. So H. StJ. Hart in *JTS* 3 (1952) pp. 66–75. The article includes several photographs of coins which show crowns of this design, and of the 'thorns' of the date-palm.
20. The find is described by N. Haas, *IEJ* 20 (1970) pp. 49–59.
21. See further I. Wilson, *Jesus: the Evidence*, pp. 126–130.
22. For an extensive survey of tomb designs in Palestine, especially around Jerusalem, with many plans and illustrations, see Finegan, *Archeology*, pp. 181–202. For Jerusalem specifically see also M. Avi-Yonah (ed), *Encyclopedia of Archaeological Excavations in the Holy Land*, vol. 2 (Oxford University Press, 1976) pp. 627–641.
23. One exception is Jacob's Well (John 4:5–6); there is no reason to doubt that this was the same well from which visitors can still drink, in the crypt below the unfinished Greek Orthodox church near Shechem.
24. For these two locations see Wilkinson, pp. 133–136, and for the 'prison', Finegan, *Archeology*, p. 154.
25. For description and pictures of the pavement see Finegan, *Archeology*, pp. 160–161.
26. The opposite views on the location of the praetorium may conveniently be seen in Finegan, *Archeology*, pp. 156–158 (favouring Antonia), and Wilkinson, pp. 137–140 (favouring Herod's Palace). For the effect of his conclusion on the traditional 'Way of the Cross' see further Wilkinson, pp. 144–151. For a more detailed argument for the location in Herod's palace see P. Benoit, 'Praetorium, Lithostroton and Gabbatha', reprinted in his *Jesus and the Gospel*, vol. 1 (London: Darton, Longman & Todd, 1973), pp. 167–188.
27. Finegan, *Archeology*, pp. 163–165, sets out the evidence for this pre-Constantinian tradition.
28. See further the discussion in Wilkinson, pp. 145–150.
29. The original proposal came from Otto Thenius in 1842.

30. Gordon's own account of his reasons is reproduced in Wilkinson, pp. 198–200; it does not inspire confidence in his historical judgement!
31. See e.g. Finegan, *Archeology*, p. 173.

Chapter 5 Jesus in History

1. See above pp. 15–16.
2. The article, 'No room for the inn?', published in *Third Way* (December 1984) p. 15, was a popularisation of a carefully-researched article, 'The Manger and the Inn: The Cultural Background of Luke 2:7', by K. E. Bailey in *ERT* 4 (1980) pp. 201–217. Bailey's case depends on the observation that in Palestine a manger is normally to be found not in a separate 'stable' but in the main living room of a peasant house, where the animals are brought in at night.
3. I have outlined the deliberate 'eccentricity' of Jesus' life-style in relation to material wealth in 'God and Mammon', *EQ* 51 (1979) pp. 6–8.
4. See especially his reaction to popular enthusiasm after the miraculous feeding of the crowd, John 6:14–15. The political significance of this incident is well brought out by C. H. Dodd, *The Founder of Christianity* (London: Collins, 1971) pp. 128–135.
5. E. P. Sanders, *Jesus and Judaism* (London: SCM Press, 1985), especially pp. 61–76, 270–271, 287; the theme recurs throughout the book. See also B. F. Meyer, *The Aims of Jesus* (London: SCM Press, 1979) especially pp. 181–185, 197–202.
6. See my discussion of 'kingdom'-terminology, 'The Church and the Kingdom of God: Some Hermeneutical Issues', in D. A. Carson (ed), *Biblical Interpretation and the Church* (Exeter: Paternoster Press, 1984) pp. 30–44.
7. See above pp. 90–91.

Index